The Niebuhr Brothers
for Armchair Theologians

Also Available in the Armchair Theologians Series

Aquinas for Armchair Theologians by Timothy M. Renick
Augustine for Armchair Theologians by Stephen A. Cooper
Barth for Armchair Theologians by John R. Franke
Bonhoeffer for Armchair Theologians by Stephen R. Haynes and Lori Brandt Hale
Calvin for Armchair Theologians by Christopher Elwood
Heretics for Armchair Theologians by Justo L. Gonzalez and Catherine Gunsalus Gonzalez
Jonathan Edwards for Armchair Theologians by James P. Byrd
John Knox for Armchair Theologians by Suzanne McDonald
Liberation Theology for Armchair Theologians by Miguel A. De La Torre
Luther for Armchair Theologians by Steven Paulson
Martin Luther King Jr. for Armchair Theologians by Rufus Burrow Jr.
The Reformation for Armchair Theologians by Glenn S. Sunshine
Wesley for Armchair Theologians by William J. Abraham

The Niebuhr Brothers
for Armchair Theologians

Scott R. Paeth

Illustrations by Ron Hill

© 2014 Scott R. Paeth
Illustrations © 2014 Ron Hill

First edition
Published by Westminster John Knox Press
Louisville, Kentucky

14 15 16 17 18 19 20 21 22 23—10 9 8 7 6 5 4 3 2 1

All rights reserved. No part of this book may be reproduced or transmitted in any form or by any means, electronic or mechanical, including photocopying, recording, or by any information storage or retrieval system, without permission in writing from the publisher. For information, address Westminster John Knox Press, 100 Witherspoon Street, Louisville, Kentucky 40202-1396. Or contact us online at www.wjkbooks.com.

Book design by Sharon Adams
Cover design by Jennifer K. Cox
Cover illustration: Ron Hill

Library of Congress Cataloging-in-Publication Data

Paeth, Scott.
 The Niebuhr Brothers for armchair theologians / Scott R. Paeth ; illustrations by Ron Hill.
     pages cm. — (Armchair theologians series)
 Includes bibliographical references and index.
 ISBN 978-0-664-23698-4 (alk. paper)
 1. Niebuhr, Reinhold, 1892-1971. 2. Niebuhr, H. Richard (Helmut Richard), 1894-1962. 3. Theology—United States—History—20th century. I. Title.
 BX4827.N5P34 2013
 230.092'2—dc23

2013031727

♾ The paper used in this publication meets the minimum requirements of the American National Standard for Information Sciences—Permanence of Paper for Printed Library Materials, ANSI Z39.48-1992.

Most Westminster John Knox Press books are available at special quantity discounts when purchased in bulk by corporations, organizations, and special-interest groups. For more information, please e-mail SpecialSales@wjkbooks.com.

Contents

Acknowledgements   vii

Introduction   ix

1. Beginnings   1
2. The Church in the World   23
3. Christian Realism   45
4. Theology in a World at War   73
5. Revelation and Responsibility   97
6. To Accept What We Cannot Change   129
7. The Niebuhr Legacy   153

Notes   175

For Further Reading   189

Index   193

Acknowledgments

I am grateful for the many people who were instrumental in the completion of this project and who aided me throughout the writing process. I owe an immense debt of gratitude to the teachers who instilled in me a sense of deep respect for the Niebuhr brothers in my theological education, particularly Max Stackhouse, Gabriel Fackre, and Mark Heim, who showed me how both Reinhold and H. Richard Niebuhr could inform theological and ethical discourse in a modern context. I am also grateful to Stephen Crocco, the librarian at Princeton Theological Seminary, for his help early on in identifying sources about the life and theology of H. Richard Niebuhr. Additionally, I am thankful for the time and generosity of those who were willing to read versions of this manuscript in various states of development, particularly those students who assured me that I was not in fact pitching over the head of my audience. DePaul University has been generous both in providing me time and resources to write and research and in providing me with a wealth of opportunities to teach and discuss the legacy of the Niebuhr Brothers. I hope that this book represents a worthwhile recompense.

Most particularly, I am grateful for the patience and indulgence of my family, who allowed me the time and space to bring this project to completion. To my wife, Amy, who was willing to read drafts of several early chapters and offer suggestions for revision, I am particularly grateful.

INTRODUCTION

Reinhold and H. Richard Niebuhr are two of the most influential American theologians of the twentieth century. Between them they have affected conversations in theology, politics, ethics, and philosophy for more than half a century, and their influence seems only to increase over time. Jointly, they may have inspired more—and more diverse—theological movements than most other modern theologians can lay claim to.

As brothers, Reinhold and H. Richard Niebuhr laid claim to the same heritage, the same lineage. They attended the same schools—Elmhurst, Eden, and Yale—and went through many of the same formative experiences together.

Introduction

And yet they responded quite differently to the moments of historical significance that they encountered in their long and active careers and focused in sometimes strikingly different ways on distinct problems in the field of Christian theology and ethics. One of the great challenges of this project was in trying to reflect how their different points of view arose naturally from their common history. At the same time, each of them recognized and honored the importance of the other's contributions, even in the midst of their occasional disagreements.

The Niebuhr brothers lived and wrote in the midst of one of the most tumultuous times in U.S. history. Their lives took them from World War I, through the Great Depression, into the crucible of World War II, through the Cold War and, in the case of Reinhold, the flux and change of the 1960s. Different as they were from one another, both recognized the need for Christian theology and ethics to be cognizant of and responsive to the questions of the time, and each took seriously his vocational responsibility to speak publicly about the central issues of the day. Their work endures not only because their insights remain fresh to this day but also because they provide a model for how to do theology in public.

Today we are in the midst of what has been called a "Niebuhr Revival," which is largely due to the rediscovery of the relevance of Reinhold Niebuhr's thought to the problems of morality and politics at the beginning of the twenty-first century. Yet to those with eyes to see, the Niebuhrs have been with us all along. Their influence underlies many of the debates that have taken place in the decades since their deaths, and theologians of every stripe have at one point or another had to contend with some dimension of their thought, either resisting or adopting it, and sometimes adopting it while claiming to resist it.

Introduction

We live, as the Niebuhrs did, in the midst of tumultuous times. We have also lived through war and economic collapse, as well as new challenges that neither of the Niebuhr brothers could have imagined in their own lifetimes; however, their theologies provide resources that may be utilized in the construction of theologies capable of responding to the tests of our time as the Niebuhrs did to theirs, aware of human frailty and limitation, yet courageously standing for justice and social responsibility in public life. What we may learn from them is not only how to think theologically about the relationship of Christianity to the problems of public life, but also how to act Christianly in response to those problems in order to strive for a relatively more just society and a Christian community committed to a center of value beyond itself.

CHAPTER ONE

Beginnings

Between them, Reinhold and H. Richard Niebuhr have wielded an influence on American Christian theology matched by few, if any, other theologians in the twentieth century. Their contributions to the creation of Christian social ethics alone merits them a mention in any history of the development of Christian thought in the modern era, but their influences extend far beyond those contributions. Reinhold's thought has held sway across disciplines as diverse as foreign policy and pastoral theology, while Richard's contributions to philosophical theology, the sociology of religion, Christian ethics, and the history of American Christianity have influenced generations. As brothers, they were lifelong collaborators and rivals, and as theologians and ethicists, they offered some of the most enduring contributions of Christian moral thought over the last one hundred years. Today, we are experiencing a "Niebuhr revival" as a new generation discovers their continuing relevance in a turbulent time.

Early Years

Reinhold Niebuhr was born on June 21, 1892, in Wright City, Missouri, the third of four children, to Gustav and Lydia Niebuhr. Richard was born two years later, on September 3, 1894. Gustav, an earthy farmer who emigrated to the United States from Northern Prussia in 1881, served for ten years as a local church pastor while also traveling extensively to aid in the work of planting German Evangelical churches across the American frontier.

The denomination to which the Niebuhrs belonged, the German Evangelical Synod, had descended from the Prussian Union Church, which combined elements of both the Lutheran and Reformed theological traditions.[1] Ecumenical and irenic by design, it sought to overcome theological conflict by an appeal to the common ground of Scripture, rather than insisting on strict adherence to one set of traditions or confessions.[2] Gustav was, in a very real sense, his childrens' first teacher of theology, instructing them in the Bible and teaching them Greek.

Gustav's approach to theology, which would later be mirrored in the work of his sons, mixed both traditional German piety with a commitment to the application of Christian faith to the pressing social issues of his day.[3] He was influenced by both the theological liberalism of

Beginnings

Albrecht Ritschl and Adolf von Harnack and the moral force of the social gospel movement.[4] He was an advocate of temperance (not always a popular stance within the German American community) and stood in favor of the kind of progressive politics advocated by Theodore Roosevelt.[5]

In 1902, the Niebuhr family moved from Wright City to Lincoln, Illinois, where Gustav became the pastor of Saint John's Evangelical Church. Lincoln was a heavily German-speaking town, and Gustav quickly became a prominent leader, working to deepen ties within the community, as well as building bridges to the non-German population of Lincoln.[6]

It was here in Lincoln that Reinhold and Richard grew into their own as young men. Their father presided in the pulpit of Saint John's, where the boys were confirmed. At home and in church, the primary language spoken by the Niebuhrs was German, while around town and at school, they spoke English.[7] This bilingual upbringing would serve them both well, as it eventually gave them a head start in reading and disseminating the cutting edge German theology of the twentieth century, particularly the works of Karl Barth and Ernst Troeltsch.

Reinhold and Richard each took on themselves aspects of their parents' personality and outlook. While they both became ministers and theologians, Reinhold was very much his father's son, fiery and outspoken, while Richard, shy and introspective, took after their mother.[8] Perhaps significantly, when it came time for them to choose a musical instrument to learn, Reinhold chose the trombone, while Richard chose the flute.[9] Their older siblings forged their own paths: Eldest brother Walter went into business and journalism, while their sister Hulda became a pioneer in the field of Christian education.

3

In 1907, at the age of fifteen, Reinhold began his studies at Elmhurst College. Today a small liberal arts college on the outskirts of Chicago, at the time it was the proseminar for the Evangelical Synod, a preparatory academy for young men pursuing a vocation in ministry.[10] Although he was an excellent student, eventually graduating as valedictorian of his class, Elmhurst's academic quality at the time left much to be desired. He graduated in 1910 and then went on to continue his theological studies at Eden Seminary. Richard graduated two years later, in 1912, and also went on to study at Eden.

There, Reinhold fell under the influence of biblical scholar Samuel Press, whose seminar on the book of Amos was to make a lasting impression on him. "All theology really begins with Amos," Reinhold proclaimed years later at a dinner in Press's honor.[11] At Eden, Reinhold contributed articles to the school's literary journal and took part in an intercollegiate debating society.[12] Richard was equally successful as a student, if less outgoing than Reinhold.

Beginnings

After graduation in 1913, Reinhold intended to continue his studies at Yale Divinity School. However, his father's untimely death put those plans in jeopardy. He took over his father's pulpit temporarily, preaching at Gustav's memorial service and serving as pastor of St. John's, but ultimately left to pursue his studies in New Haven the following September.

"A Mongrel among Thoroughbreds"

At Yale, Reinhold quickly found himself in a challenging new environment, both academically and socially. What Elmhurst and Eden had lacked in scholarly rigor, Yale more than made up for, and Reinhold quickly rose to the challenge. He confided in Samuel Press, however, that he felt

underprepared and overmatched by his peers, writing in a letter that he felt like "a mongrel among thoroughbreds."[13] His inferiority complex was rooted, not only in regional and class differences, but also in a genuine sense that he had been deprived of much of what was valuable in a traditional liberal arts education through his provincial schooling.

Despite his misgivings, he thoroughly immersed himself in his studies at Yale and was particularly captivated by his classes with D. C. Macintosh, who introduced him for the first time to the pragmatism of William James, a philosophical influence that would shape much of his future thought.

James was one of the founders of pragmatism and wrote on a wide variety of issues ranging from psychology and the theory of knowledge to the nature of religious experience. Central to James's philosophical outlook was the belief that "truth" as an idea was not defined by reference to an objective point independent of human experience but was rather defined by its practical consequences. "Truth is what works," James argued.[14] In other words, ideas, if they are to be understood as true, make a concrete difference in our lives and in our actions. To affirm a belief in the truth of something is to have a stake in its validity and usefulness for human life. James was interested in knowing the "cash value" of truth—why it mattered in terms of human experience.[15]

Another key aspect of James's approach to pragmatism was his emphasis on the importance of religious experience. One of his most influential books, *The Varieties of Religious Experience*, attempted to understand religion not as the study of the dogmas of religious institutions but rather in terms of the experiences of religious adherents.[16]

Under Macintosh's influence, Reinhold found in James's philosophy both an intellectual basis for his own increasingly modernist religious outlook and an antidote to moral extremism, which would serve him well in formulating his own conception of Christian realism.[17] His Bachelor of Divinity thesis, supervised by Macintosh, defended James's pragmatic approach to certainty in religious knowledge against the positivism of French philosopher August Comte and the idealism of G. W. F. Hegel.

Despite his affinity for a Jamesian approach to pragmatism, Reinhold was nevertheless critical of the excessive optimism of some pragmatists, as well as the pragmatic tendency toward relativism.[18] Furthermore, he recognized a tendency in pragmatism to treat empirical questions as though they could be abstracted from the context in which they were analyzed, without reference to the particularities of those engaged in observation.

Nevertheless, the critical stance that pragmatism provided Reinhold gave him a basis for a theological ethic that was both always under revision and constantly on the watch for the kinds of unjustified brands of idealism and

utopianism that were to become the chief foils of his Christian realist approach to morality.[19]

Reinhold returned to Yale the next year to continue his studies. He completed an MA degree in 1915, writing his thesis once again under D. C. Macintosh. This thesis focused on the doctrine of immortality in Christian theology, contrasting the Hebraic and Christian conceptions of immortality to the understanding more prevalent in the Greek philosophical tradition. His work reflected the influence of Ritchl's theology within the Yale community, an influence that affected Reinhold no less than his mentors.[20]

Reinhold was offered the opportunity to study for his doctorate at Yale but chose instead to take a pastoral position. His obligations to both his church and to his family made it impossible for him to continue his studies.[21] He took up a position as pastor of Bethel Evangelical Church in Detroit, Michigan, in August of 1915.[22]

Richard at Elmhurst and Eden

Richard, meanwhile, followed Reinhold, first to Elmhurst, then to Eden, and finally to Yale. At the same time, however, he was forging his own path as a theologian and ethicist. After graduating from Elmhurst in 1912, he too studied with Samuel Press at Eden.[23]

Richard shared with Reinhold a disdain for what they both perceived to be the backward and out-of-date education they had received at their denominational schools.[24] Early on, Richard began pressing the Evangelical Synod to bring its educational system more in line with American academic standards, including a more rigorous liberal arts education and instruction in English.[25]

After graduating, he went on to work for a year as a reporter for his brother Walter's newspaper in Lincoln

Beginnings

(which would also serve as the venue for many of Reinhold's early writing endeavors) before being ordained as a minister in 1916.[26] He received a pastoral call to Walnut Park Evangelical Church outside of St. Louis, where he served for two years. At the outbreak of the First World War, Richard enlisted in the army as a chaplain, but the war ended before he was deployed.[27] During his time at Walnut Park, he continued his education, eventually earning an MA in German from Washington University.[28]

In 1919, Samuel Press, by then the President of Eden Seminary, extended to Richard an invitation to teach theology and ethics at his alma mater.[29] During his time there, in the aftermath of World War I, the Evangelical Synod began moving toward a greater integration in American society, particularly in its adoption of English as a standard of instruction. At Eden, Richard lectured solely in English.[30] In 1920, he married a woman from Lincoln named Florence Marie Mittendorf, whom he had first met in his father's congregation. They would eventually have two children, Cynthia and Richard Reinhold Niebuhr, who would himself one day become a prominent American theologian and professor at Harvard Divinity School.

Meanwhile, Richard continued to press forward in his studies. In addition to continuing work at Washington University, he enrolled in summer classes at the University of Michigan and the University of Chicago, a practice Reinhold referred to as "academic vagabondage."[31]

In 1922, Richard gave up his vagabond life and enrolled full time at Yale Divinity School. While continuing pastoral work, he completed a BD and a PhD at Yale. Here again, as with Reinhold, D. C. Macintosh was a major influence. Richard's dissertation, completed under Macintosh's direction, was titled "Ernst Troeltsch's Philosophy of Religion."[32]

What James was for Reinhold, Troeltsch was for Richard: a major intellectual influence whose work had an impact on all of Richard's future work. Along with Max Weber and Emile Durkheim, Ernst Troeltsch was a founding father in the field of the sociology of religion. His major work, *The Social Teaching of the Christian Churches*, was a massive exploration of the relationship between Christian churches and their social contexts.[33]

Troeltsch developed a typology through which he divided Christian communities into three broad categories, "churches," "sects," and "mystical groups."[34] The church, according to Troeltsch, is "overwhelmingly conservative, . . . to a certain extent accepts the secular order, and dominates the masses." As a result, he argued, it becomes "an

Beginnings

integral part of the existing social order."[35] The sects, by contrast, are smaller, voluntary associations geared more toward the inner perfection of believers rather than the validation of the status quo. They are not primarily concerned with justifying and supporting the society and may at times come into conflict with it. As a result, the church is the bulwark of the ruling class, while the sects are associated with the lower classes. Mystical communities form around what Troeltsch refers to as "a purely personal and inward experience."[36] As a result, they have little staying power as social organizations and don't wield much influence on the development of religious institutions. This typology,

particularly the church/sect distinction, became central to Richard's understanding of American religious life.

Richard completed his PhD in 1924 and was invited to take up the presidency of Elmhurst College. He set upon an ambitious plan to reform the curriculum of his old school, updating, enhancing, and "Americanizing" it. He raised the academic standards of the school, launched new fundraising and campus construction initiatives, and began phasing out German-language instruction.[37] Beyond this, he shook the established status quo by arguing that Elmhurst should begin accepting women as students and broadening the curriculum to include students who were not interested in pursuing a vocation in the ministry.[38] Seeking to create links with the other small colleges in the area, he began to chip away at the walls of ethnic enclosure that the Evangelical Synod had constructed around its educational institutions.[39] In 1927 he returned to Eden as its academic dean.

Taming a Cynic

Reinhold, meanwhile, had risen to prominence as both a writer and as a pastor in his adopted city of Detroit. From his arrival in 1915 to his departure for Union Theological Seminary in 1928, Reinhold applied his prodigious energies to his pastoral duties on the one hand and to his burgeoning career as a popular writer, political activist, and commentator on the other. During his time there, Bethel Church grew from sixty-five members to over six hundred.[40] In part, this was due to the explosive growth of Detroit itself, which was in the midst of becoming the center of the automotive industry in the United States, but it was also due to the passion and fire that Reinhold brought to the pulpit.

Reinhold was not at first particularly happy at Bethel. He viewed himself as a "callow young man" who had little to offer the members of his church.[41] Coming back to the Midwest and pastoring this small "mission church" was not what he had in mind when he first ventured off to Yale, and he found himself ill at ease with many of the Evangelical Synod pastors in the Detroit area, with whom he had little in common, least of all in their enthusiasm for the German cause in the First World War.[42] Like Richard, Reinhold saw the continuing emphasis on German identity as an obstacle to overcoming the divisions between his church and the broader community of American Christianity. In a conscious act of defiance against the old guard, Reinhold became an ardent American patriot.

However, it was more than just the tensions within the Evangelical Synod that led to his frustration, and Reinhold found much of the daily work of pastoring a church daunting. He often avoided the work of pastoral visitation and after a short time admitted that his sermons were becoming repetitious.[43] He admitted that little of his prior theological education really prepared him for the actual tasks of ministering to a community. "Where," he wrote, "did anyone ever learn in a seminary how to conduct or help with a Ladies Aid meeting?"[44]

Nevertheless, he set himself to the work of pastoring to the people of Bethel with what often seemed to be a sort of grim determination. Aware of his many shortcomings as a minister, he also knew that the church and his congregants were a responsibility that he could not take lightly. And this knowledge motivated him to persevere even in the face of his limitations.

His mother was a great help to him in this. After moving to Detroit to live with Reinhold, she immediately began

The Niebuhr Brothers for Armchair Theologians

directing the Sunday school and the choir. As an experienced pastor's wife, she helped guide Reinhold in his early years at Bethel, and her expertise allowed him to begin devoting a greater portion of his time to writing and, eventually, out-of-town traveling and speaking engagements.[45]

One of his first major pieces of writing was a cover story for *The Atlantic* titled "The Failure of German Americanism," which reiterated many of the frustrations he had felt for years with his denomination and his ethnic community.[46] He described the German American community as moribund and conservative, unwilling to change for the sake of integrating into the U.S. mainstream. His argument, as might be expected, was not warmly accepted throughout the German American community, but it did establish him as a talented and provocative writer.[47] *The Atlantic*, along with other liberal magazines such as *The New Republic* and

Beginnings

The Nation, became frequent publishing venues for him. During this period, he also began writing frequently for *The Christian Century*, which encouraged him to send them whatever he had.[48]

With the United States' entry into the war in 1917, Reinhold became involved in the Evangelical Synod's work to maintain contact with its members serving in the military.[49] He briefly considered joining the army as a chaplain but was talked out of it by the Synod's president.[50] He nevertheless remained an enthusiastic supporter of the American cause throughout the war.

Remaining in Detroit, he continued the work of pastoring to his growing community at Bethel church. As the community grew, so did Reinhold's prominence and influence in Detroit. He leveraged that prominence to speak out

against the working conditions at Henry Ford's automotive factories and on behalf of the rights of workers to organize.[51] His preaching embodied much of the spirit of social gospel liberalism that was prominent in the mainline churches of that era.[52] He was also an early advocate for the rights of Detroit's African American community, working with community leaders to improve conditions in impoverished black neighborhoods and seeking to improve their working and living conditions.[53]

It was also during this period that Reinhold first began to discover the importance of the Jewish voice in the struggle for social justice. He once recalled the Episcopal Bishop Charles Williams telling him "there are only two Christians in Detroit, and they are both Jews."[54]

After the war, Reinhold joined a delegation to Europe led by YMCA leader Sherwood Eddy. In a series of dispatches written for *The Christian Century*, he described with horror the desolation of the postwar continent, the abuses endured by the conquered Germans at the hands of the French, and the toll that the draconian postwar policy of reparations was taking.[55] These experiences both began to inform his nascent understanding of the tensions between moral idealism and political realism and utterly disillusioned him regarding his earlier enthusiastic support for the war, leading him to declare that "this is as good a time as any to make up my mind that I am done with the war business."[56]

For much of the 1920s, Reinhold's intensive schedule of preaching, pastoring, writing, and traveling kept him on the move. He would often travel during the week, only to arrive back in time to preach his Sunday sermon. Sometimes he would stay up all night to finish an article for *The Atlantic* or *The Christian Century*. His prodigious body of work, his success as a pastor, and his popularity as a speaker came of his seemingly endless supply of intellectual energy and intensive work ethic.

In 1927, Reinhold published his first book, *Does Civilization Need Religion?*[57] While it has not aged as well as some of his later work, it nevertheless exhibits many of the themes that became prominent in his later work. It reflects his social concerns as well as his commitment to social gospel principles of justice, equality, and peace. At the same time, one can see even here the emergence of the skeptical anthropology that would later undergird much of his criticism of the naivety of the social gospel movement.

Does Civilization Need Religion? had the effect of expanding Niebuhr's audience and brought to him an invitation to join the faculty of New York's Union Theological Seminary, whose President, Henry Sloane Coffin, was in the process of expanding the faculty and returning the focus of the seminary to the preparation of students for ministry.[58] Coffin extended his invitation despite the fact that Reinhold did not hold a doctorate. Due to funding issues, however, the position was initially only to be part-time. Kirby Page, editor of the Christian socialist journal *The World Tomorrow*, was eager to have Reinhold working and writing with him in New York, and he and Coffin agreed to "share" Reinhold, splitting his time between teaching at Union and an editorial position at Page's journal. And so in 1928, after thirteen years as the pastor of Bethel Church, Reinhold resigned his position and set out for New York. A year later, he began teaching at Union full time.

Reinhold's second book, *Leaves from the Notebook of a Tamed Cynic*, published in 1929, is unique among his writings in that it is not a work of theology per se, but rather consists of diary excerpts from his years at Bethel. As a record of his years in the pastorate, it makes for fascinating, and sometimes surprising, reading.

The book makes no grand theological arguments, but reflects the experiences of a young pastor finding his way in the midst of the often-difficult work of Christian ministry. It also charts the development of Reinhold's thinking regarding an array of social issues, from economic justice and the aftermath of the First World War to ecumenical relationships among Christians and interfaith interactions between Christians and Jews. More significantly, however, it demonstrates his honest struggles with his own identity as a pastor and a preacher, his struggles with both the theological and practical demands of his life, and his interactions with the members of his congregation.

What one comes to understand in reading *Leaves* is the way in which Reinhold, who came unhappily to his pulpit in 1915, came over the course of thirteen years to enjoy and embrace his pastoral vocation. In its final pages, one can see Reinhold beginning to articulate a distinction between his own way of thinking and the forms of sentimental idealism

with which he would ultimately break rather strongly. In seeking to find a path that embraced both a principled adherence to the ethic of the gospels and a commitment to making a practical difference in the social conditions of the world, he is beginning, near the end of this book, to articulate the tensions between the fact of human self-interest and the possibility of self-transcendence that would come to be central to his thinking in the coming decades.

From Eden to Yale

Upon his return to Eden, Richard continued to press for the increased integration of the Synod into the larger American society. Like Reinhold, he was increasingly influenced by the social gospel movement and pushed the denomination to become more attentive to questions of social justice that had previously been neglected.[59] He was sympathetic to the labor movement, but at the same time he argued while at Elmhurst that the Christian vocation of the school was served as well by graduating students who would apply Christian teaching to the world of business as by those who would enter the ministry.[60] Following in the tradition of social gospellers like Walter Rauschenbusch and Washington Gladden, both Niebuhr brothers were pushing their denomination to do more than simply ameliorate the ills of society, but in fact to "Christianize" the social order.[61]

Richard also threw himself into the burgeoning ecumenical movement, working with the Evangelical Synod to overcome the divisions between denominations and even move toward mergers among the various warring factions of Protestant Christianity.[62] This work laid the foundation for what in 1934 became the Evangelical and Reformed Church.[63]

In addition to his administrative and denominational work while at Eden, Richard was at work on what would become his first major publication. In 1929, he published *The Social Sources of Denominationalism*, with which he would begin to make his mark on American Christian theology. The following year, he took a sabbatical from Eden, most of which was spent in Germany. Reinhold joined him near the end of his trip, and the two brothers traveled to Russia with Sherwood Eddy.

Their experiences of Soviet Russia impressed both brothers deeply. Each sent back dispatches to the United States reporting their experiences. Reinhold wrote a series of articles for *The Christian Century* while Richard's accounts appeared in the *Evangelical Herald*.[64] Both were sympathetic to socialism and saw potential in the creation of a socialist society. They both saw in the Soviet Union for the first time what appeared to them to be a viable alternative to a capitalist economic system, one that opened up new possibilities for social justice.[65] Yet they were also both suspicious of the hardline Marxist ideology espoused by the communist party and sought a brand of pragmatic, nondoctrinaire socialism that would be compatible with their Christian commitments. In the end, both recognized that

Soviet-style socialism could not be compatible with the Christian gospel, but both came back to the United States more determined to participate in the creation of an American brand of socialism.[66]

Upon arriving back in the United States, Richard was invited to join the faculty of Yale Divinity School. In 1931, he and his family moved to New Haven, where he took up the academic position that would define the remainder of his theological career.

CHAPTER TWO

The Church in the World

By the time H. Richard Niebuhr had arrived at Yale in 1931, he had already made a major mark on the field of Christian ethics and the sociology of religion with *The Social Sources of Denominationalism*. In the next decade, however, his contributions would continue to grow, and his theological perspective would become more clearly defined, both in terms of his fraught relationship with the social gospel movement and in distinction from his brother.

The Church within the Churches

The Social Sources of Denominationalism opens with a characteristically Niebuhrian expression of wit. "Christendom," Richard writes, "has often achieved apparent success by ignoring the precepts of its founder."[1] Richard's ambitious goal in his first book was to demonstrate, following in the footsteps of Ernst Troeltsch, Max Weber, and R. H. Tawney, the relationships between the theological and sociological dimensions of Christianity. His central argument, which emerged at least partly from his own struggles to overcome the ethnic provincialism of the Evangelical Synod, was that Christian denominationalism was much more directly related to the social and economic circumstances of the churches than it was to theological or doctrinal particularities.

Denominationalism, as Richard analyzes it, is a betrayal of Christian unity, which he argues was central both to the teaching of Jesus Christ and the writings of the early biblical authors. It is, he writes, "an unacknowledged hypocrisy, . . . a compromise, made far too lightly between Christianity and the world."[2] Denominationalism justifies and solidifies divisions on the basis of class, race, and ethnic background, allowing the privileged and the powerful to segregate themselves from the lower and working classes while justifying their own position on doctrinal and theological grounds. Richard observes acidly that "it was easier to give Caesar the things belonging to Caesar if the examination of what might belong to God were not too closely pressed."[3]

Richard views his task not simply as a descriptive exercise in sociology, but as an ethical critique of the church. Denominationalism is not a morally neutral category for understanding divisions between churches, but rather, it is evidence of a willingness to compromise the spirit of the gospel in ways that undermine the moral purity of Christ's teaching. The rigor of the gospel—it's radicalism—is undermined by the ease with which Christians are complacently willing to accept the existence of a caste system within the very structure of the Christian community itself.

Relying heavily on Troeltsch's "church/sect" typology, Richard identifies the central problem of the Christian church as the failure of the "church" type bodies, oriented toward the preservation of the status quo and the protection of their own authority and prerogatives, to respond to the social circumstances of the oppressed and the disinherited. As the Church curries favor with the privileged and powerful, the lower classes respond by creating their own voluntary, separatist communities, which are more directly responsive to the needs of their members. These communities abandon the structure, ritual, and authority of the

church-type institutions, substituting direct religious experience, moral purity, and a "bottom up" authority structure. Richard writes:

> The evil of denominationalism lies in the conditions which makes the rise of sects desirable and necessary: in the failures of the churches to transcend the social conditions which fashion them into caste-organizations, to sublimate their loyalties to standards and institutions only remotely relevant if not contrary to the Christian ideal, to resist the temptation of making their own self-preservation and extension the primary objective of their endeavor.[4]

That Richard frames this as an "ethical failure" is a clue that he is not interested in simply offering a sociological analysis of the development of denominationalism in the United States, but is rather engaged in a project of Christian social ethics. By investigating the social conditions that produced the multiplicity of American denominations, he is attempting to demonstrate that the doctrinal arguments that appear to be at the root of denominational splits often mask the deeper social divide between the privileged and the powerless.

Denominationalism has a cyclical quality, as sectarian groups transform over the passage of time into churches and once again accommodate themselves to serving the privileged. As the first voluntaristic, charismatically inspired generation gives way to its children and grandchildren, the community ceases to embody the values of the sect, particularly the importance of religious experience, exclusivity, and the priesthood of all believers. Furthermore, as they enter the "establishment," they adjust their ethics to accommodate the social conditions that benefit the maintenance of the status quo. They become "respectable" and put aside

The Church in the World

the more radical implications of their sectarian forebears. While the sects "prefer isolation to compromise," the churches are inclusive, supporting the "national, cultural, and economic" interests of the society of which they have become a part.[5]

The result of these divisions is that Christianity has become "ethically weak" and incapable of aiding in the development of a socially just and moral society, beset as it has become by arguments over the proper response to social crises, such as wars and economic downturns. With the memory of the First World War fresh in his mind, Richard writes that the churches "usually join in the 'Hurrah' chorus of jingoism, to which they add the sanction of their own 'Hallelujah'; and, through their adeptness at rationalization, they support the popular morale by persuading it of the nobility of its own motives."[6] In the face of this ethical

weakness, the churches lack the resources to respond prophetically, becoming an arm of the socially powerful and failing to stand for a genuinely Christian morality.

One complicating factor in the American context is the existence of the "color line": the stark line of division between white and black churches. Unlike most of the other denominational divisions in the United States, almost nobody pretends that there are legitimate denominational differences that divide the white churches from the black. On the contrary, the racial motivation for that division is manifest and comprehensible. At the same time, it is one of the most transparent demonstrations of the moral failings of Christian denominationalism, embedding the history of racial segregation in the midst of the Christian community and ignoring the admonition of the apostle Paul that "in Christ there is neither Jew nor Greek."[7]

Divisions between white and black churches are clearly, Richard argues, "anthropological, not theological" and fundamentally rooted in racial prejudice and doctrines of white supremacy that have their origins in the slave trade. The earliest slaveholders were suspicious of attempts to evangelize slaves because they understood that it was immoral for Christians to hold other Christians as slaves. Ironically, it was often missionaries who created moral justifications for slaveholding as a means of getting the masters to allow them to preach to their slaves.

Even so, for much of the early history of the United States, there was not a division between slave and free when it came to worship. Slaves worshiped in the same churches as their masters, though often segregated. In part, this was so that their masters could ensure that they received an approved version of the gospel message, and in part to prevent the emergence of an educated and independent class of black clergy. It was in the wake of the Civil War that

The Church in the World

distinctly African American denominations began to appear in earnest.

While decrying the continuing racial segregation of the churches (a division that remains a widespread problem), Richard acknowledges that the emergence of African American denominations was an important step forward in the struggle of former slaves for equality with their former masters. They were now allowed to organize their own communities, with their own leadership, and preach a gospel that was not sanitized for the protection of white privilege. Nevertheless, he argues that such segregation can only be, at best, a temporary state, necessary to secure genuine equality between white and black Christians. On the other hand, he states "something more than a sociological cure is necessary for the healing of this wound in the body of Christ." Claims by white Christians that there is no distinction between Jew

and Greek are often heard as ironic or even hypocritical, "but sometimes there is in it the bitter cry of repentance."[8]

To overcome the divisions within Christianity and respond relevantly to the social situation, Richard argues, it is necessary for Christianity to reembrace the ethic of the gospels, the creation of a community of love "in which each individual can realize the fully potentiality of an eternal life in self-sacrificing devotion to the Beloved Community of the Father and all the brethren."[9] This requires the acceptance of an ethic of moral stringency that includes an insistence on the love of neighbor and enemy, an ethic of nonviolence, and the rejection of nationalism in the name of universal brotherhood among Christians. It also requires the reaffirmation of the social ideal of the early church in which "distinctions between rich and poor will be abrogated by the kind of communism of love which prevailed in the early Jerusalem community."[10]

Such a community, he argues, is not simply another sect, but rather would exist, as it always has, as a "church within the churches."[11] It would not need to branch off into a new movement of purity but would remain within its communities, as a spirit of renewal and transformation that would continue to affirm an ethic rooted in the love and reconciliation that is at the heart of the gospels. Such a movement may not change the world, at least not all at once, but it can work within the denominations as an impetus to overcoming their divisions, and within the Christian community to at least partially redeem those communities through its call to repentance.

The Church against the World

At Yale, Richard immersed himself more fully in the major texts of the Christian tradition. Jonathan Edwards began to assume a major role in Richard's thought, as did Søren Kierkegaard.[12] As the Great Depression deepened, Richard's thought began to turn to the failure of the church to respond robustly to the economic crisis and its accommodation of the complacent Christianity of the middle classes. His next major work, *The Church against the World*, written as a series of essays with Wilhelm Pauck and Francis Miller, built in some ways on the closing pages of *The Social Sources of Denominationalism* and began to consider the need for the church to detach itself from a society that had far too successfully coopted it for the sake of the rich and powerful.

Western Christianity, he argues, is held in captivity to cultural forces from which it needs to be liberated. The church has compromised with the prevailing culture to the degree that it has lost sight of its Christian identity. As Christians have come to associate their Christian faith with a particular nation or economic system, they have become engaged in acts of idolatry, substituting a temporal and finite reality for the true, transcendent reality of God. Similarly, to the extent that Christianity has become about human self-fulfillment, rather than about the crucified and resurrected Christ, it has ceased to be the church. He writes: "It is a church which seeks to prove its usefulness to civilization, in terms of civilization's own demands. It is a church which has lost the distinctive note and earnestness of a Christian discipline of love and has become what every religious institution tends to become—the teacher of the prevailing code of morals and the pantheon of social gods."[13]

The solution to this captivity of the church is a revolt in the church against its dependency on an anthropocentric, nationalist, and capitalist society. In part, such a revolt has already taken place, he argues, among those who see the church's captivity to the existing order of society and

conclude that the true nature of the church is that of a moribund traditionalism or romanticism on the one hand, or tyrannical despotism and support for the powerful at the expense of the disenfranchised on the other. This revolt *against* the church, however, is a revolt of those who are not genuinely loyal to the church as it is intended to be, but have loyalties to principles and interests apart from the church.

The revolt *within* the church must take place among those who recognize that the church in captivity to culture is not what it is intended to be. They are loyal, he says, "to the essential institution while they protest against its corrupted form."[14] They are not seeking to change the church into a stalking horse for some other movement or institution, but seek to change it back to its original form and restore it to its essential mission. This revolt is "a revolt both against the 'world' of contemporary civilization and against the secularized church."[15]

The Church in the World

Echoing the themes of *The Social Sources of Denominationalism*, Richard points out that the church has in its history repeatedly allied itself with cultural forces that then bent it to their own aims, whether it be the Roman Empire, the feudal system, or the domination of the southern states by the North. "In every instance," he writes, "the result was a new tyranny, a new disaster and a new dependence of the church."[16] Even movements based on the highest ideals of Western society, such as liberty, equality, and fraternity, which themselves originated in the teaching of Christianity, make the fundamental mistake of thinking that these ideals can be established by temporal power and the use of force, and as such are simply another form of the same kind of captivity from which Christians must liberate themselves.

And yet, this puts Christians on the horns of a dilemma: To support social revolution is to risk becoming captive to it; but to refuse to participate is itself a capitulation by the church to its captivity to the current status quo. It is necessary for the church to declare its independence from these competing brands of political coercion in the name of its own deepest principles. Such a declaration of independence requires of the church a "withdrawal" from attempts to actively engage the world in a process of transformation.[17] It is not, in other words, a revolt of the church *within* the world, but a revolt *against* the world. The purpose of such a withdrawal, however, is precisely to enable the church to escape its bondage to the secular world so that it may reengage in the process of social transformation, but now properly rooted in the gospel proclamation of Jesus Christ. Such a liberation, he writes, is for "the sake of a new aggression and a new participation in constructive work."[18]

In order for Christianity to reengage society, it must remember that its first obligation is not to a particular social vision or even to the creation of a better society per se, but rather to God. The Church's loyalty to God trumps any loyalty to the movements, ideals, or institutions for social change that it might otherwise ally itself with. Only by maintaining that loyalty to God is it possible for the church to engage society on its own terms without succumbing to bondage to society and accommodating itself to society's demands: "If the church has no other plan of salvation," he writes, "to offer to men than one of deliverance by force, education, idealism, or a planned economy, it really has no existence as a church and needs to resolve itself into a political party or a school."[19]

At the same time, Richard is quick to note that the God in whom Christians believe is the necessary foundation for human life and society is not only the God of judgment and destruction, but also, and fundamentally, the God who became incarnate in Jesus Christ. It is through the crucified Christ that we come to understand the way in which God is the Lord upon whom we are ultimately dependent. A

church that has become dependent on the dominant culture will reject and ignore the message of Christ crucified, while a church rooted in the deepest commitments of the Christian faith will make the cross central to its life, action, and message.

By reaffirming its commitment to a Christianity rooted in the gospel proclamation of the crucified Christ, the church can liberate itself from its captivity to a culture that is committed to the imposition of political solutions through force and coercion in a way that is antithetical to Christ. By articulating the ideals of the gospel over the ideals of worldliness, the church can engage in revolt against the injustice of a world dominated by nationalism, capitalism, and humanism while at the same time not being co-opted by precisely those cultural forces that they are aiming to defeat.

In many ways, Richard's essays in *The Church against the World* represent an ethical elaboration on many of the themes of *The Social Sources of Denominationalism*. In the prior volume, he had traced the pattern of renewal and assimilation that has taken place repeatedly in the church over the centuries, while in *The Church against the World* he pleads, as he did near the end of *Social Sources*, for a sustained movement of renewal in the church that will not run the risk of being once again absorbed into the predominant cultural milieu in which it finds itself.

A Kingdom Without Judgment

As the Great Depression ground on, Richard was looking for a way to provide a firmer theological foundation for the ideals of the social gospel. It was not to be found, as he argued in *The Church against the World*, by wedding the mission of the church to the cultural fashions of the day, but had to be sought in an authentically Christian articulation of the nature of the moral life and of society. In *The Kingdom of God in America*, Richard takes issue with a social gospel reading of history that sought to justify its idealism by rooting it in the origins of American Christianity. "It was simply impossible," he writes, "to force Puritans, Quakers, and the great leaders and movements of the eighteenth and early nineteenth centuries into the mold of the modern social gospel."[20] On the contrary, Richard argues, for these early American Christians the kingdom of God implied not only the establishment of divine justice in the world but the imposition of divine judgment against human arrogance and idolatry.

The idea of the kingdom of God, he argues, does not mean only one thing in American Christianity, but develops over time. In the early colonial period, the kingdom of God referred to the "sovereignty of God," while in the midst of the great awakenings of the eighteenth and nineteenth centuries it meant the "reign of Christ." It was only in the late nineteenth and early twentieth centuries that it had come to be understood as the "kingdom on earth."[21] And yet these three conceptions of the kingdom are interdependent, and no adequate conception of the kingdom of God can be developed without the presence of all three dimensions.

America was, for Protestant Christians, a refuge from the religious upheavals of Europe in the aftermath of the Reformation. It represented a realm of freedom where there were neither ecclesiastical authorities nor repressive governments to restrain and obstruct their attempts to reconstruct Christianity in light of their Protestant principles. As such, it became a laboratory for what Richard calls "an experiment in constructive Protestantism."[22] Thus the goal from the start among Christian communities in the new world was not simply to detach themselves from their communities of

The Church in the World

origin, but, as one Puritan divine put it, "to practice the positive part of the church reformation, and propagate the Gospel in America."[23]

The central social problem for the early American protestant communities was the attempt to organize their common life in response to this doctrine of divine sovereignty. While the Bible was understood in some way to provide the basis for this, there was by no means any consensus on how it could be so. To place too great an emphasis on the biblical revelation undermined the idea of God's living sovereignty over human lives. While the Puritan colonists tended to resolve this tension by a sort of biblicism, the Quakers strongly emphasized the authority of the living spirit of God. Both were attempting to understand the way in which divine sovereignty offered a basis for the creation of a common social life. In a similar vein, the Protestant emphasis on the independence of the church was rooted in its understanding of God's sovereignty and the freedom of the

Christian community from all institutional constraints save those imposed on it by God.

While the early Protestant community in America was motivated by faith in God's sovereignty, as Christianity took root in the new world, the emphasis began to shift to the kingdom as the kingdom of Christ. This motif had always been present, though in a secondary way, among the early Puritan colonists, but it came to the forefront of American Christianity with the first Great Awakening. The emphasis moved from obedience to the divine command to the regeneration of the believer's soul and from fear of the Lord to reconciliation in Christ. As Richard points out, this motif did not overthrow the earlier emphasis on God's sovereignty, but was rather predicated on it. Whether in the theology of Jonathan Edwards or George Whitefield, John Wesley or Archibald Alexander, "faith in the divine sovereignty was the platform on which they stood as they preached the kingdom of Christ."[24]

What this meant in the moral lives of believers was an emphasis on repentance and self-restraint, overcoming the power of evil within their own lives. Spiritual restoration in Christ required the overcoming of the power of the flesh and a conversion of the ego from sin and rebellion against God, demonstrating that they as believers could be open to the love and forgiveness of God and could be enabled to love and forgive one another. In political life, this tended to produce a renewed move toward separatism, as individual virtue supplanted the early Puritan concern with a well-ordered society. To be sure, there were political implications to this shift, but the emphasis on changed hearts and lives drew the Christian community away from the direct application of a constructive Christian approach to life in the political arena.

The third motif in American Christianity, however, was much more strongly inclined toward social and political

The Church in the World

reform. The emphasis on the coming kingdom of God, while muted in the earlier Puritan movement and in the midst of the Great Awakenings, became much more central in the eighteenth and nineteenth centuries. It was impossible, Richard argues, to read the Bible without acknowledging that God's judgment and promise carried with it social as well as individual implications. Christian hope was never solely for a kingdom beyond this world, but within the world as well: "The kingdom of prophetic vision was moreover a coming kingdom, not one that lay beyond the vale of tears. Men were hastening toward it, but it was hastening toward them with even greater urgency."[25]

The coming kingdom, far from being the peaceful realm of liberal sentimentalism, was a threat of destruction against everything that human beings sought to value for their own

sake apart from God. It "was the fruition not only of divine goodness but of human badness in conflict with that unconquerable goodness."[26] But this was only half the story, for the coming kingdom was also a promise of peace, joy, and harmony in the overcoming of human evil. The rise in millennialism in the wake of the Great Awakening is rooted in this apocalyptic expectation of a rising tide of evil before God's coming kingdom arrives, but this millennialism was itself an extension of the prior motifs of divine sovereignty and the kingdom of Christ reigning in the human heart rather than an expectation of a particular sequence of biblically foretold apocalyptic events. But even so, the expectation was of a kingdom on earth, as it is in heaven, and not just a heavenly expectation.

This motif, Richard argues, comes into its own in the nineteenth century. During this century the expectation of the coming kingdom manifested itself, Richard argues, in manifold ways, and not all positive. It can be detected in forms of humanism and nationalism, which secularize its expectation of social change and the renewal of life and divest it of its emphasis on divine sovereignty and the power of Christ to change the heart. It can also be found in doctrines of national and racial superiority, most obviously in the doctrine of Manifest Destiny, and associated with the rise of industrial capitalism. The American Civil War was motivated in part by the millennial expectation of a coming kingdom, as Richard notes with dry irony: "When the new day came it was no reign of peace and brotherhood: it was called Reconstruction. Instead of the supper of the Lord in the kingdom of heaven America celebrated its 'Great Barbecue.'"[27]

The social gospel movement at its best, represented by figures such as Washington Gladden and Walter Rauschenbusch, incorporated the earlier motifs without which a doctrine of the coming kingdom was emptied of moral and spiritual content. Thus their vision was not solely for a renewed society but for regenerated hearts responsive to a sovereign God. Richard writes:

> In all their search for the redeeming word which might direct misery on the way to joy, turn injustice toward righteousness and send warring men down the paths of peace, Gladden, Rauschenbusch, and their colleagues carried with them a vision and a promise which had been written not on stone or paper but on the fleshly tables of the heart by a fresh and nation-wide experience of the resurrection. Their fathers believed that Christ was risen from the dead and was in the midst of men not only because they had read the story of the empty tomb . . . they believed because they had seen. . . . So their children were directed to march in their own time toward the coming kingdom not by a rationalism which regarded cross and resurrection, redemption and atonement, as ancient superstitions, or by liberalism which denied the divine sovereignty, but by their memory of a loyalty to the kingdom of God, which has not been ashamed of the gospel.[28]

This evangelical expectation of the coming kingdom that motivated the early social gospel, however, had been replaced by a sentimental liberalism that saw the coming kingdom, not as the manifestation of God's sovereign reign in Christ, but as the fulfillment of human potentialities and expectations. It had been institutionalized and divested of its religious content, even among Christians, and as a result had lost its prophetic edge. It became simply another manifestation of national identity or economic class. Prophetic preaching was replaced by bland moralism and naive optimism, and the dialectic of hope and judgment in the idea of the kingdom was abridged, leaving any notion of divine wrath by the wayside. Thus, as Richard famously describes American Christianity: "A God without wrath brought men without sin into a kingdom without judgment through the ministrations of a Christ without a cross."[29]

The Kingdom of God in America in many ways continues to make the case of *The Church against the World*, insofar as it describes the process of institutionalization and domestication of Christianity, depriving it of its status as a movement, as a dead end from which the church must escape by rediscovering its identity as a movement dedicated, first and foremost, to the gospel of Jesus Christ and obedience to a sovereign and loving God. The mistake of the church in identifying itself with cultural trends and powerful interests at the expense of the gospel had created an American Christianity that expected to build the kingdom of God with human hands, and with no suffering, and which needed to remember that the cross is set against all of humanity's attempts to make itself God.

Richard was developing a conviction that, as he states in *The Kingdom of God in America*, Christianity "must be understood as a movement rather than as an institution or series of situations. It is gospel rather than law, it is more dynamic than static."[30] When the church seeks to establish itself as an institution, and particularly when it affiliates with the interests of the powerful within society, it loses the dynamism that sustains it and becomes a moribund apologist for the social status quo. As a movement it is always involved in the process of history, and should never be content to rest on a false synthesis, but always remember its own partial and incomplete character. A truly "catholic" church, he argues, is an impossibility from within a human framework, since no human society or institution can possess a genuinely universal point of view, yet he contends

The Church in the World

that, particularly in America, what Christianity needs "is recovery of faith in the invisible catholic church."[31] Such a faith can empower Christians to engage in a realistic struggle with the moral issues that it confronts rather than rely on sentimental bromides, putting its confidence finally and solely in "a sovereign, living, loving God."[32]

CHAPTER THREE

Christian Realism

In 1928, Reinhold Niebuhr resigned his pastorate at Bethel church in Detroit to take a position teaching at Union Theological Seminary in New York. By this time, he was nationally known as a theologian, preacher, and political commentator. Union was an ideal venue from which to continue his engagement with questions at the intersection of religion and public life and became the locus for many of the major transitions he would undergo in the coming years.

His time in Detroit had allowed him to develop his skills as a speaker, writer, and analyst of events. He had come a long way from the "callow young fool" who had first stepped into the pulpit of Bethel Church thirteen years earlier. Detroit had come a long way as well, having become the hub of the U.S. auto industry, the epicenter of much of the social upheaval and transformation that would reverberate across the nation in the coming decades and that would contribute to the transformation of Reinhold's own theological outlook as well.

Reinhold in New York

Reinhold proved to be a popular figure among Union's students, who flooded to his lectures and sermons, as well as his impromptu commentary sessions after meals in Union's common room.[1] He developed a reputation as a dynamic speaker, often lecturing extemporaneously from a brief outline in his classes.[2] "Reinie," as his students referred to him, remained deeply enmeshed in politics and writing. His writing was sometimes prescient, such as in identifying key causes of the Great Depression the year before it struck. He also endorsed nonviolent direct action as a strategy for overcoming Jim Crow laws in the South.[3]

In 1928, he endorsed Norman Thomas, the perennial Socialist Party candidate, for president. Thomas represented a nondogmatic approach to socialism, which appealed to Reinhold's own nondogmatic sensibilities. His move to New York also began an intellectual and political shift in his understanding of Christian social responsibility, one that would eventually lead to his embrace of a particularly Christian brand of political and social realism. In 1930, he took his first dip into the waters of electoral politics, running for State Assembly as a Socialist and losing badly.

That was also the year that Reinhold met Ursula Keppel-Compton, a student at Union. While Reinhold's frenetic schedule had seemed to preclude any possibility of

Christian Realism

ultimately settling down to marriage, the young English woman managed to pierce his defenses. They announced their engagement at the end of that academic year, before Ursula set sail to return to Great Britain. He joined her briefly during the summer holidays and returned for the wedding in December of 1931.

Ursula became, in many ways, Reinhold's partner and collaborator from then on. An excellent theologian in her own right, she acted as a support and sounding board for Reinhold as he developed the ideas that would become the basis for his later major publications. At the same time, his hectic work schedule did not relent. In the winter of 1931, fresh from his wedding, he continued to travel across the country preaching and lecturing, while at the same time writing and fulfilling his teaching responsibilities at Union. In the midst of all of this, he continued to work toward building the Socialist Party as a radical alternative to the more complacent liberalism that he found increasingly bothersome within the social gospel movement. Reinhold's political work would lead him to his second run for political office in 1932 as a candidate for Congress on the Socialist Party ticket, which he also lost badly.[4]

During this period, the shift in his thinking about Christian responsibility within society was becoming increasingly apparent. As his politics became more radical and militant, his distance from his fellow liberal Christians increased.

Breaking with the Social Gospel

The root of Reinhold's shift can be seen in his increasing dissatisfaction with what he saw to be the complacent and naive idealism of much of the social gospel movement. Since his time in Detroit, Reinhold had been active in movements for social reform and against war. But Detroit

The Niebuhr Brothers for Armchair Theologians

also taught him hard lessons about the difficulty of achieving social progress in the face of resistance by the powerful. Moral suasion by itself was often ineffective at creating change. Power had to be met with countervailing power in order to force change where necessary.

For many of Reinhold's liberal Christian associates, however, social change was desirable only to the degree that it could be brought about through exclusively Christian means. For them, this meant rejecting force as an option and relying solely on their power to move the consciences of those they wished to persuade. Reform could not be brought about through coercion, but required changing the hearts and minds of the powerful.

Reinhold began to argue that such an approach would never result in change, but simply allowed the powerful to remain in power while salving the consciences of those

Christian Realism

Christians who wanted social change but didn't have the stomach for the kind of fight it would take to achieve it.

The problem, he began to see, was the conflict between what it took to be effective in the political realm and the kind of moral purity on which the social gospellers insisted. Politics, as they say, ain't beanbag. By insisting that they remain above the fray of genuine political conflict, moralizing from on high, the social gospellers were betraying the very goals that they claimed to be supporting, making it easier for the powerful to exploit the vulnerable, and refusing to advocate the kinds of remedies that real social change required. Force, even violence, in the name of justice was a necessity that liberal Christians were as yet unwilling to embrace, even for the sake of the goals they advocated.

Reinhold began to embrace a social analysis that had more and more in common with Marxism while still pursuing the more reformist agenda of the social gospel. He was less interested in Marxist calls for revolution and the overthrow of the bourgeoisie than he was in its understanding of the way in which ideologies could mask the use of power for the sake of domination. A Marxist analysis revealed how the sentimental idealism of the social gospel actually helped to prevent the establishment of genuine social justice; at the same time, however, Reinhold's goals were still, in large measure, the goals of the social gospel movement.

However, Marxism could never be a final answer for Reinhold. If the social gospel made the mistake of naively believing that Christian ideals were sufficient to overcome social problems, Marxism erred in its Promethean belief that human beings were capable of creating a new society wholly through their own efforts. Marx was a Christian heretic in that his brand of communism was essentially a form of messianic Christianity, but without God. Both

Marxists and the social gospellers believed that they could establish the kingdom of God on Earth, but the Marxists understood, better than the social gospellers, what the political realities of that transformation might be. Both, however, failed to take account of the limitations of human prospects in actually bringing that about.

Niebuhr Versus Niebuhr

An exchange between Reinhold and Richard in the pages of *The Christian Century* in the spring of 1932 is indicative of the direction Reinhold's thought was taking and the increasing distinction between the approaches of the two brothers. The catalyst for their conflict was a dispute among many liberal Christians over the proper response to Japan's invasion of Manchuria in September of 1931. For Christian pacifists, the situation created a dilemma. On the one hand, they were outraged over Japan's actions, but on the other, they were morally committed to a stance that condemned any coercion as contrary to Christian morality.

Christian Realism

There were Christians, including Reinhold, who believed that the situation demanded some form of definitive response. They supported moves to declare an embargo on Japan in order to force a withdrawal from Manchuria. Others suggested a boycott against all Japanese products. There was a recognition on the part of those advocating these approaches that they could lead to further escalation and perhaps even war, but they did not believe that they could stand aside and allow Japan's aggression to go unanswered.

Nobody, least of all Reinhold, was advocating military action. Their recommendations were purely economic, and to an extent symbolic. And yet they were clear that their goal was to force Japan to capitulate, and this overtly coercive approach was what gave pause to many of the pacifist supporters of the social gospel.

Richard's position, as laid out in his *Christian Century* article, "The Grace of Doing Nothing" sought to frame the question in light of a faith in the sovereignty and providence of God.[5] His argument echoed themes that he had earlier begun to develop in *The Church against the World*: that the Christian community has to understand itself, not as a participant within a set of unjust social institutions but as an alternative rooted in an ethic of repentance and forgiveness.

Richard begins by distinguishing between different ways of doing nothing. Not all types of inactivity are created equal. There is the inactivity of the pessimist, who expects the world to fall apart and is unsurprised when it begins to do so; and there is the conservative inactivity of those who support the status quo, who believe that aggression like that perpetrated by Japan is no different from the action any nation would take, and who wait only for the opportunity for their nation to do likewise. There is also the inactivity of the frustrated and outraged pacifists who, having renounced violence and coercion, find themselves incapable of

responding effectively to a situation where some form of coercion may be the only effective course of action. "Having tied his own hands he fights with his tongue and believes that he is not fighting because he inflicts only mental wounds."[6] Finally, there is the inactivity of the communists, who expect a new world to arise from the conflicts of the present situation and whose inactivity does not reflect an abject despair, but hope for the future. It is an intentional inactivity rooted in a realistic appraisal of the way political conflicts arise and are resolved.

While all of these ways of doing nothing are meaningful in their own way, all fail to take into account the possibility of the present action of God in the midst of human affairs. This form of inactivity is rooted in a faith that affirms, with the communist position, that a better future is arising out of the conflicts of the present, but that, in distinction to the impotent inactivity of pacifist idealism, sees that future as resting entirely in God's hands, and not solely as the product of human moral action.

History, Richard argues, is the record of both judgment and redemption. God is bringing about the divine plan for the world irrespective of human desires, and "our wishes for a different result do not in the least affect the outcome."[7]

> This God of things as they are is inevitable and quite merciless. His mercy lies beyond, not this side of, judgment. This inactive Christianity shares with communism also the belief in the inevitably good outcome of the mundane process and the realistic insight that the good cannot be achieved by the slow accretion of better habits alone but more in consequence of a revolutionary change which will involve considerable destruction.[8]

In the face of God's inevitable and inexorable judgment, Christians may have no recourse to action that will change the situation as it stands, but that does not mean that there is not work to be done. Rather the Christian task is to begin to construct an alternative community. Richard refers to such communities as "cells" and envisions a Christian international organization, analogous to the Communist International, which could embody the spirit of a radical Christian alternative to an ethic of the cultural status quo.

Such a Christian community could embody the spirit of Christian repentance and forgiveness within a society in which those ideas are distinctly counter-cultural. In doing this, these Christian communities would embody a spirit of hopeful anticipation of a kingdom of God, not to be brought about by the continual moral improvement of human society, but by the sovereign action of God.

In his response to his brother, Reinhold begins by acknowledging much of Richard's argument. He sees Richard as attempting to distinguish his understanding of Christian ethics from the naivety and sentimentalism of liberal theology.[9] For Reinhold, however, the central problem was not that of a Christian community that did not know how

to "do nothing" constructively, but rather the impossibility of love as the basis for a social ethic. According to Reinhold, the chief flaw in Richard's analysis is his simultaneous identification of the tragedies of history with the "counsels of God" and his expectation of God's coming kingdom.[10]

For Reinhold, a Christian social ethic needs to take account of the necessity for action in the context of human limitations and frailty. In short, the problem for Reinhold is the conflict between love and sin. "I find it impossible," he writes, "to envisage a society of pure love as long as man remains man."[11] Society can be improved, and human behavior can be made to conform more closely to the ideal of pure love, but it can never achieve it. To achieve a just society, he argues, will always require some degree of coercion, albeit ideally only the minimum necessary. Richard seems to believe that God will "introduce something into

Christian Realism

history which is irrelevant to anything we find in history now," and that, Reinhold argues, cannot serve as a foundation for ethical action.[12]

The key difference that Reinhold sees between his own position and Richard's is that, for Reinhold, "the history of mankind is a perennial tragedy" whereas Richard "wants religion and social idealism to deal with history."[13] But this requires an absolutism, he argues, that is incompatible with a life lived in the flux of history. "Man cannot live without a sense of the absolute, but neither can he achieve the absolute."[14] And this paradox is central to the tragic view of history as Reinhold perceives it, as well as to the moral imperative to act in the absence of assurances of the purity of one's action.

Richard's brief response focuses on the central theological difference between the two brothers, namely: Is God, or

is God not, involved in history? Reinhold views God as outside the historical process, while Richard views God as involved in history in the deepest and most fundamental ways:

> He is the structure of things, the source of all meaning, the "I am that I am," that which is that it is. He is the rock against which we beat in vain, that which bruises and overwhelms us when we seek to impose our wishes, contrary to his, upon him.[15]

War and human conflict are the action of God only as a consequence of the human insistence on them. God does not inflict war on us. We inflict it on ourselves, but it stands as the judgment of God on our sinful and self-seeking behavior.

Rather than a perennial tragedy, Richard views history as a "road to fulfillment" that "requires the tragic outcome of every self-assertion" so that love might reign.[16] The tragic view may ultimately produce a kind of harmony, he argues, but only that of the domination by the strong of the weak. In that sense, he argues, Reinhold may be right. In a world of unmitigated tragedy, a pacifism rooted in the expectation of a fulfillment of human hope by a sovereign God would leave the weak and vulnerable to be exploited by the powerful.

Ultimately, Richard argues, it is a choice: "either the Christian method, which is not the method of love but of repentance and forgiveness, or the method of self-assertion; either nationalism or Christianity, either capitalism-communism or Christianity. The attempt to qualify the one method by the other is hopeless compromise."[17]

Reinhold and Richard agree, in this sense, in their condemnation of a brand of complacent and self-satisfied liberal Christianity that objects to the use of force but believes

Christian Realism

that it can cure human ills through the exercise of love. For Reinhold, this implies that the ideal of love must yield to the imperatives of justice, and Christians must take the side of the weak and oppressed against the powerful. For Richard, on the other hand, it requires human beings to stop attempting to impose their will on God and building false utopias, but rather to get down into the weeds and do the hard work of preparing the ground for the coming kingdom of God, which in the end is God's action and not something that human beings do on their own or the world's behalf.

What is striking about this exchange between the two brothers is not simply that they offered very different prescriptions for Christian moral action in the world, but that those prescriptions grew out of the same ground—a disillusionment with the love, idealism, and naivety that had

become central to so much of the social gospel movement by the early 1930s. Both brothers perceived clearly that whatever the way forward for Christian ethics might be, the remedies proposed by the liberal Christianity that had been so influential for both of them were no longer effective for dealing with the pressing issues of their time, if indeed they had ever been.

Moral Man and Immoral Society

This argument was at the heart of Reinhold's next major publication, *Moral Man and Immoral Society*, which he wrote over the summer of 1932 and which was published the following December.[18] Reinhold's increasing dissatisfaction with the complacency and ineffectiveness of many Christian pacifists was coupled by an increasingly strong insistence that the problems of social justice that confronted society could not be solved by an ethic of pure love, but required a willingness to engage in coercion.

The central theme of *Moral Man and Immoral Society* was the disjunction between the individual capacity for morality and that of groups. While it is possible for individuals to act selflessly, groups are incapable of exercising the same kind of self-giving love. Political action requires coercion because not only will the powerful refuse to relinquish their power voluntarily, but they will also establish putatively moral justifications for why they are entitled to wield it. This problem is innate to any social group, even those that claim to speak for the disenfranchised. As he argued in his dispute with Richard, pure love in social relations is not a human possibility, though relative forms of justice may be possible. Even in striving for social justice however, it is only possible to reduce, but never totally eliminate, self-interest or coercion.

Christian Realism

Group identity both gives focus to the sense of individual self-importance and founds its interests in the moral impulse to self-sacrifice. Forms of group identity, such as nation, race, and class, appeal to our instincts of both self-assertion and self-sacrifice. We both subordinate our good to a larger cause and identify our good with that cause. In this sense we are never free from egoism; we simply project it onto larger and larger screens.

Central to Reinhold's argument in *Moral Man and Immoral Society* is the recognition that appeals to moral principle can at the same time motivate the best within us and provide a mask for the worst within us. This is as true of the religious resources we bring to politics as it is of our rational resources. While religion can motivate individuals to act in the name of high principle, it can also be co-opted as a tool of oppression. It can justify resistance to evil, and it can justify the evil itself. Perhaps worse, religious perfectionism can become an excuse for political defeatism, as idealists afraid of tainting their moral purity retreat from the messy fray of political conflict. In withdrawing from the world, they preserve their sense of pristine righteousness, but at the cost of allowing injustice to reign unchallenged.

On the other hand, the religious liberals of the social gospel movement commit an equally grave mistake in assuming that love can provide a governing moral principle of political life. Politics operates in the realm of power and coercion, which Reinhold argues are contrary to love. The highest principle of political life is therefore not love, but justice, and even that principle is often honored more in the breach than the observance. What love may motivate individuals to do will not motivate larger groups. As Reinhold states:

> The weakness of the spirit of love in solving larger and more complex problems becomes increasingly

apparent as one proceeds from ordinary relations between individuals to the life of social groups. If nations and other social groups find it difficult to approximate the principle of justice, as we have previously noted, they are naturally even less capable of achieving the principle of love, which demands more than justice.[19]

To expect political life to be governed by appeals to love, he argues, is dangerously sentimental and ignores the reality of a political system that is oriented toward grasping and holding onto power.

None of this is to say, however, that idealism does not play an important role in political life. Both rational and

religious idealism, Reinhold argues, "qualify" political life. But, he continues, "this qualification can never completely eliminate the selfish, brutal, and antisocial elements, which express themselves in all inter-group life."[20] As Reinhold argued against Richard, the ethic of love that stands at the heart of Christianity is ultimately a tragedy in the political realm, even as it is the highest moral ideal of individual life. The cross stands as the symbol of both the tragedy and triumph of that ideal, but it cannot serve as the basis of a political morality. "The cross," he writes, "is the symbol of love triumphant in its own integrity, but not love triumphant in the world and society. Society, in fact, conspired the cross. Both the state and the church were involved in it, and probably will be so to the end."[21] By transforming love into a political slogan, he argues, liberal Christianity has stripped it of its apocalyptic implications while at the same time leaving themselves unarmed for the real struggles of political life.

The practical implication of this for Reinhold is that Christians need to shed their illusions and take part in political activity, even potentially violence, for the sake of securing equal justice in society. The privileged classes will never relinquish power voluntarily through the use of moral suasion. A realist political strategy must be willing to utilize political force, even revolution, in order to compel the privileged to hand power over to the oppressed. To stand apart from the fight in the name of high principle is to abandon the claims of justice and stand implicitly on the side of the powerful against the interests of the weak.

Despite his criticisms of liberal moralism, however, Reinhold continued to insist that morality played a role in political life. Democratic reform, he argues, is preferable to violent revolution. It is more likely to achieve a just form of socialism through the political process, as the examples of Great Britain and other European democracies demonstrate:

> The hope that socialism could be achieved progressively by parliamentary action has at least been partially justified by the history of all these nations. . . . Everywhere the state has interfered in the processes of economic society with the purpose of diminishing the privileged and restraining the power of the owners, and adding to the privileges and power of the workers. . . . In this whole development we may discover the unusual combination of moral and coercive factors that are evident in political change when violence is avoided and pressure is exerted in purely political terms. The various abridgements and diminutions of the social privilege and power of the owners are accomplished partly by the political power which is exerted by the workers; but there is always an element of voluntary acceptance of the new social standard because it appeals to the total community as a logical and inevitable extension of previously accepted political and social principles.[22]

Democratic systems can achieve, through their relatively moral processes, a greater degree of social assent from even those members of society who are disadvantaged by the achievement of some measure of justice because they have assented to the political process that produced the results.

Realism, Reinhold argues, must always be tempered by morality, while at the same time moral idealism has to come to terms with its limitations in the political sphere. The achievement of moral ends in conditions of political conflict requires the use of force as a means, though not necessarily violent force. This was something, Reinhold argues, that Gandhi understood well. His struggle for justice in India was not, as it was seen by many liberal Christians, based on

purely moral action, but was rooted in the necessary coercion of the powerful in order to force them to give up their privilege. Gandhi's genius was not that he achieved political progress without coercion, but that he was able to effectively coerce his political opponents without resorting to violence. The difference, however, between nonviolent coercion and overt violence is, Reinhold argues, not one of kind but of degree. Nonviolent coercion is still coercion and thus still stands in contradiction to the Christian ideal of wholly self-giving love. Reinhold endorses nonviolent resistance as a strategy for achieving social justice both in India and in the civil rights struggle in the United States, arguing that "non-violence is a particularly strategic instrument for an oppressed group which is hopelessly in the minority and has no possibility of developing sufficient power to set against his oppressors."[23] This insight is at the heart of Martin Luther King Jr.'s strategy of nonviolent resistance in the American South two decades later.[24]

The Niebuhr Brothers for Armchair Theologians

The core of Reinhold's argument is the paradoxical relationship between love and justice, individual and society, idealism and realism in the political realm. These concepts are indelibly intertwined with one another yet stand in tension. Love is necessary in the pursuit of justice, as idealism is necessary to temper a cynical form of realism. But when love is made a substitute for justice, or idealism a replacement for a realistic appraisal of circumstances, individual morality is mistaken for a social agenda, and as a result love leads to the defeat of justice, and idealism is conquered by a realism that cares solely for power at the expense of morality. However, when love and justice stand in tension with one another, justice becomes the approximation of love in a world where love in its pure form is impossible.

His next publication, *Reflections on the End of an Era*, built on some of the themes of *Moral Man and Immoral Society*. Reinhold sharpened his analysis of the way that ideology, particularly class ideology, masks self-interest and provides cover for economic injustice. As the Great Depression deepened, with no relief in sight, Reinhold's radicalism also deepened. *Reflections* offers some of Reinhold's most overtly Marxist and least overtly religious arguments. He summarizes the argument of the book thusly:

> The political power in any society is held by the group which commands the most significant type of non-political power, whether it be military prowess, priestly prestige, economic ownership or the ability to manipulate the technical processes of the community. If the governing group is able to add to this possession of power an implicit confidence in itself as the rightful government, a high morale and a sure sense of direction it is able to win the consent of the rest of the community to its rule and maintain it without challenge. The governing group either believes itself

Christian Realism

to be or tries, at least, to create the illusion that it is, ordained, either by some mystical "divine right" or by an only slightly less mystical "consent of the governed," to hold the reins of power in society and to symbolize the unity of the nation. The ability of a governing group to transmute its specialized nonpolitical power into political power depends on the plausibility of its claim to government and the willingness of society to accept that claim.[25]

While Reinhold was always clear about the deficiencies of Marxism as a political program, in *Reflections on the End of an Era* we see him embracing Marxism as a method of analysis more clearly than anywhere else in his work. The emphasis on the way in which the powerful and privileged use ideology in order to seize and maintain control owes a great deal to Karl Marx's class analysis, and while Reinhold does not share with Marx the principle that the working classes are immune to the dangers of misusing ideology, we

can see here echoes of Marx's famous dictum that "the ruling idea of every era are the ideas of the ruling class."[26]

Yet while Reinhold may not have been focusing on the theological foundations of his moral case in these books, it was never far from the surface, and in his next book he made them explicit.

The Impossible Possibility

In *An Interpretation of Christian Ethics*, Reinhold sought to ground his burgeoning Christian realist analysis of morality and society more directly within the Christian ethical tradition.[27] Central to his argument in this book is the distinction he draws between the "prophetic" ethic of Jesus and a merely prudential ethic that views morality primarily in consequentialist terms.

Prophetic religion, which stands at the core of both Judaism and Christianity, is characterized by its emphasis on the transcendent, which "is the power which lifts religion above its culture and emancipates it from sharing the fate of dying cultures."[28] Other religions are culturally bound and lack the ability to conceive of themselves as having an independent existence apart from the world from which they emerge, whereas prophetic religion, because its source stands outside of time and history, can sustain itself and survive in the midst of social and cultural upheaval. Connected with this is the ability of prophetic religion to achieve a measure of independence from moral and political trends, since its point of reference is not that which surrounds it, but that which stands apart from it.

Yet, as Reinhold later argues in *Beyond Tragedy*, we are always "deceivers, yet true," in the sense that all our attempts to speak truthfully about Christian faith are inescapably symbolic expressions of a reality that cannot be fully

Christian Realism

captured within human speech.[29] There is no way to reduce Christian truth to a set of simple rational assertions. Rather, we express its truth through mythology, through poetic and artistic expression, and through symbol and ritual. We are "deceivers" in the sense that we can never speak with complete truthfulness about the nature and character of God because it transcends human capacity for expression. But we are "true" in the sense that, in our attempts to speak of God, we are speaking of the ultimate reality that grounds human existence.

The role of the prophet is always to bring the hard word to the rulers, reminding them that God is always greater than even their most elevated accomplishments and stands in judgment over our inevitable moral compromises. This is what distinguishes the true from the false prophet: "The mark of false prophecy is that it assures the sinner peace and security within the terms of his sinful ambitions. True

prophecy has the function of revealing the true laws of life to the sinner, and discovering to his blind eyes how he increases his insecurity by taking the law into his own hands for the purpose of establishing himself in an insecure world."[30]

The ethics of Jesus, Reinhold argues, represents a perfection of that prophetic tradition, which expresses the ideal of suffering love in its purest form, and therefore at the same time becomes an "impossible possibility" within history—so morally pure as to be incapable of realization in the context of human social life. At the same time, however, such an ethic is crucial to dealing with the social problems of modernity since it both points beyond itself to a transcendent "source of meaning" and yet avoids the temptation to escape the world by becoming absorbed into the "eternal world where all history ceases to be significant."[31] Prophetic Christianity thus stands between a morality that seeks to escape the world and one that is tempted to become completely immersed in it. Christian ethics holds both sides of this equation in tension with one another by recognizing human life as being simultaneously related both to the temporal and the eternal.

The ethics of Jesus encapsulate this tension precisely because they are grounded in a faith in the creative unity of God on the one hand and in the goodness of the created world on the other. But his ethics do not revolve around trying to achieve some form of relative good in the world that satisfies the collective interests of society. Precisely because the ethics of Jesus rejects the egoistic basis of what Reinhold terms "naturalistic" ethical systems, it is not interested in questions of balancing relative goods. Rather, it is wholly focused on the question of obedience to the loving will of God. But God's love, unlike human ethical systems, is wholly impartial and self-giving. It asks for nothing in return and requires nothing from humanity. As God in

Christian Realism

God's graciousness sends the sun to shine on both the evil and the good, as Christians we are to love our enemies and forgive those who have injured us, not because doing so will produce some particular result, but because through doing so we reflect God's love and grace in the world.

The mistake made by liberal Christians is in understanding Jesus' ethic as a form of prudential morality, which can serve to establish social justice or achieve peace through the conversion of others. The ethics of Jesus are not, in this sense, a "social" ethic, oriented to the horizontal axis of the world. It is "not an ethic which can give us specific guidance in the detailed problems of social morality where the relative claims of family, community, class, and nation must be constantly weighed."[32] It is oriented solely along the vertical axis, toward obedience to God.

Niebuhr criticizes Christian liberals for seeking to apply the teaching of Jesus directly to the problems of contemporary society, but at the same time, he is not arguing that Jesus' ethic has no bearing on the horizontal plane. Rather, he argues that the "impossible ethical ideal" of Jesus is

relevant to how societies understand the "nicely calculated less and more" of the moral life.[33]

If the self-giving love of which Jesus spoke is an "impossible possibility," in what way is it relevant? Reinhold argues that, by providing a transcendent reference point for all merely prudential ethical systems, Christ's ethic provides a basis for a hope that goes beyond the egoism of naturalistic ethical systems and recognizes that all life is connected to the transcendent:

> In genuine prophetic Christianity the moral qualities of Christ are not only our hope but our despair. Out of that despair arises a new hope centered in the revelation of God in Christ. In such a faith Christ and the Cross reveal not only the possibilities but the limits of human finitude in order that a more ultimate hope may arise from the contrite recognition of those limits. Christian faith is, in other words, a type of optimism which places its ultimate confidence in the love of God and not the love of man, in the ultimate and transcendent unity of reality and not in tentative and superficial harmonies of existence which human ingenuity may contrive. It insists, quite logically, that this ultimate hope becomes possible only to those who no longer place their confidence in purely human possibilities. Repentance is thus the gateway to the Kingdom of God.[34]

The impossible ethical ideal of Christian ethics thus exposes the way in which human self-interest and sin invade even the most morally elevated attempts to ground morality in the human condition, whether those attempts are modern liberalism or Marxism. The particularities of our own perspective will lead us to assume our own moral righteousness and the evil of our opponents without allowing us the

Christian Realism

capacity to recognize the limitations of our own perspectives.

The principle of justice represents an approximation of the ideal of love in the midst of our fallen circumstances. Perfect justice is no more a possibility of the human condition than is perfect love, but the ideal of equality is more capable of realization in human experience than is love, since justice can be embodied within law, whereas love, by its very nature, transcends all law. Therefore he states, "it is impossible to construct a social ethic out of the ideal of love in its pure form."[35]

The task of Christian social ethics is not to achieve the ideal, but to strive for pragmatic approximations of the ideal given the realities of human sin and moral evil. To the degree that society can more and more closely approximate genuine equality, it will reflect the love ethic of Jesus projected into the public realm.

Though love is not a possibility for societies, Reinhold argues, echoing the main theme of *Moral Man and Immoral Society*, it is still possible for individuals. We cannot rely on political action or social institutions to act lovingly, but as individuals, we can recognize ourselves as unconditionally obligated to others, and as such we possess the potential to act in complete selflessness for their sakes. Furthermore, it is possible to continually expand the circle of our concern for others to embrace greater and greater numbers of the human family, as "every achievement of human brotherhood suggests both higher and broader possibilities."[36] The highest form of Christian moral action is forgiveness, through which the self-giving dimension of love is most fully realized. We are capable of forgiveness, and of bearing the evil done to us by others, precisely through the recognition of the evil in ourselves.[37] We are ultimately in solidarity

The Niebuhr Brothers for Armchair Theologians

with all others precisely in our sin. The moral perfection embodied in the teaching of Christ is impossible for us, as it is for everyone else, despite the modernist optimism that believes that corruption can finally be abolished from society.

CHAPTER FOUR

Theology in a World at War

Both Reinhold and Richard Niebuhr had been watching the rise of the Nazi party in Germany with growing distress for several years. Through their connections in Germany, as well as Reinhold's frequent globe-hopping trips to Europe, they kept well abreast of the growing threat that Hitler posed to peace. Less clear, however, was what the response of the American Christian community should be. Both brothers were committed pacifists at the beginning of the 1930s, and while Reinhold moved more definitively throughout the decade in the direction of what would become Christian realism, he continued for some time to advocate for an official American stand of neutrality with regard to the possibility of war in Europe.[1]

This did not, however, stop him from offering a stern rebuke to the German Christian churches, which he viewed as having a responsibility to act not only against the Nazi takeover of the churches, but against the rising currents of anti-Semitism in the country.[2] His distress grew with the advance of Nazi power across Europe. By the time he arrived in Great Britain to give the Gifford Lectures in April of 1939, preparations for a war were in full swing.[3] In April, he met with his former student Dietrich Bonhoeffer, who in addition to updating him on the increasing probability of war, also asked Reinhold to help him secure an invitation to teach at Union Theological Seminary.[4] Reinhold's experience on the ground in England, speaking with church and political leaders and seeing clouds of war growing on the horizon, affected his own stand. He came back from England determined to fight for all possible support "short of war."[5]

He also arrived home determined to challenge the pacifism and isolationism of much of the American liberal Christian establishment, including former supporters and allies such as C. C. Morrison.[6] His chief instrument in this mission was a new journal, intended to serve as an interventionist rival to Morrison's staunchly pacifist *Christian Century*.[7] Dubbed *Christianity and Crisis*, the journal, whose editorial board included not only Reinhold, but also Union Seminary president Henry Sloane Coffin and their colleague Henry Van Dusen, became the embodiment of the Christian realist position on public policy questions during the war years. The first issue, published in February of 1941, took direct aim at the pacifist position, arguing that Nazi tyranny "may result in consequences even worse than

Theology in a World at War

war."[8] He argued in a similar vein in *Christianity and Society* that "enslavement to tyranny is worse than war."[9] For the sake of the survival of civilization, Christians needed to be willing to stand strongly against the forces that would destroy it. Reinhold urged passage of the Lend-Lease Act in order to ensure that vital aid reached the British.

Christianity and Society was the new moniker for Reinhold's other journal, which until 1940 had been called *Radical Religion*. The name change reflected the changes in Reinhold's own political and economic positions during these years. The radicalism of *Reflections on the End of an Era* had faded with the implementation of many of Roosevelt's New Deal policies, as had Reinhold's commitment to the Socialist party. He resigned his membership in the spring of 1940 in response to the party's insistence on a platform of neutrality in the war.[10] Richard had made the move from the Socialists in support of Roosevelt in

1936. Reinhold ultimately viewed Roosevelt as the "lesser of two evils" in the political struggles of the day, but it took the Nazi threat to prompt a definitive break with socialism. Thus, as Reinhold's politics moved from radical to broadly liberal, so too did *Radical Religion* take on a less strident title.

The Dangers of Idealism

In 1940, Reinhold published *Christianity and Power Politics*, in which he argued forcefully against both the brand of liberal utopianism exemplified by *The Christian Century* and other organs of liberal protestant officialdom on the one hand, and the cynical pessimism of communists and other proponents of "power politics" on the other. Reinhold attempted to unmask the pretensions of both camps in order to press the United States into a more active engagement on behalf of Great Britain.

The theme to which Reinhold returns repeatedly in this collection is the danger posed by American Christian idealism and naivety in the face of the Nazi threat. From the outset, he takes aim at the prevailing antiwar sentiment among liberal Protestants. "Why the Christian Church is Not Pacifist" is a broadside against the kind of sentimentalism that he saw as motivating the refusal among the leadership of the Christian churches to advocate support for the British. A Christian ethic that attempts to understand human nature solely on the basis of an ethic of pure love demonstrates a misunderstanding of both human nature and the teaching of Jesus Christ. Such an ethic, he argues, fails to recognize "that man is a tragic creature who needs divine mercy as much at the end as at the beginning of his moral endeavors."[11]

Theology in a World at War

Reinhold labels liberal protestant advocacy of a form of "love perfectionism" as a practical political program a "heresy" and contrasts it with an approach to Christian pacifism that is more faithful to the teaching of Jesus Christ. This form of pacifism does not make the mistake of believing that society can be made more just through better and better applications of the law of love. On the contrary, it recognizes that evil cannot be completely overcome within history, and stands as a witness to the possibility of a kingdom of God that transcends history. It recognizes the tragic character of human historical reality, but by standing outside of the political fray and refusing to use violence as a tool to achieve its aims, it testifies that there is a deeper reality that stands in judgment on the world as it presently is. It would rather give love than receive justice, and so it cannot play a part in the balancing act between competing claims of power.

Liberal Christian pacifism, by contrast, fails to recognize this distinction and instead believes in the Christian ethic of love as a tool for the pursuit of justice. It thus attempts to utilize an ethic of nonresistance as a means of moral suasion in political conflict in order to overcome the resistance of its opponents. This form of pacifism, Reinhold argues, falsely assumes itself to be rooted in biblical teaching:

> Presumably inspired by the Christian gospel, they have really absorbed the Renaissance faith in the goodness of man, have rejected the Christian doctrine of original sin as an outmoded bit of pessimism, have reinterpreted the Cross so it is made to stand for the absurd idea that perfect love is guaranteed a simple victory over the world, and have rejected all other profound elements of the Christian gospel as "Pauline" accretions which must be stripped from the "simple gospel of Jesus."[12]

A realistic assessment of the human condition leads to the recognition that we are in continual violation of the gospel ethic, which is rooted in a complete trust in God that frees us from the need to act out of anxiety about our lives, as well as a love of our neighbors that requires complete self-giving. The truth of human sin and egoism is precisely that such self-giving love and total trust in God are impossible to achieve on a societal level. But ignoring this reality means that, in liberal pacifism "a morally perverse preference is given to tyranny over anarchy (war)."[13]

Reinhold recognizes the need for a democratic civilization rooted in the cosmopolitan values of liberal universalism as a necessary precondition for the creation of a just society, even as he wonders whether such a value system is "not too simple a creed to suit the complexities of our tragic era."[14] He states:

Theology in a World at War

The liberal culture which is unable to assess the relation of force to reason, to understand the coercive element in all political life, and to appreciate the "ideological" taint in all human reason when the interests of the reasoner are involved is compounded of the characteristic prejudices of academics and businessmen. In this compound is usually an admixture of denatured Christian perfectionism. This religious perfectionism has reduced Christian pacifism, which in its pure form knows martyrdom to be its end, to a council of prudence.[15]

Liberal Christian pacifism thus misunderstands both its own pedigree and the situation in which it finds itself, and so offers a political prescription that, Reinhold argues, replaces the qualified optimism of Christian faith with a "superficial harmony" that does not possess the adequate

tools for responding to the crisis posed by National Socialist nihilism.[16]

Richard at War

While Reinhold did not hesitate to advocate for strong and decisive action against the Axis powers, Richard was more circumspect. Reinhold's writings were concerned chiefly with what was to be *done*, while Richard was more interested in the question of what the war *meant*. His reaction to the war reflected his own theology and personality in much the same way that Reinhold's reflected his. And as in the earlier case of the Manchurian crisis, the central question that Richard sought to answer was "what is God doing in the midst of our situation" rather than "what should we be doing?" It was only possible, Richard believed, to answer that second question when we had arrived at an answer to the first.

In an address to the Fellowship of Socialist Christians in 1941, Richard expressed his position that "the religious issue in any particular time and place is less an issue about the specific content of actions than of the context in which each specific action is to be carried out."[17] Christian political involvement should be rooted neither in baptizing particular political or economic arrangements, such as democracy or socialism, nor of standing apart from the political system entirely, but of "organizing and shaping their political actions that they will express confidence in and loyalty to the Father of Jesus Christ and faith in the forgiveness of sins."[18] The key task of Christian ethics is the discernment of what actions most fully conform to this principle.

This is not to say, from Richard's point of view, that purity of motive is the only consideration that Christians need to bring to their actions. On the contrary, since all Christian motivations are mixed, and everything is to some degree touched by sin, we cannot wait to act until we are sure of our own purity of motive. But knowing our motives are mixed allows Christians to act in recognition that God may nevertheless act through our impure motives in order to bring about God's purposes. Therefore Christian ethics has to concern itself not only with the question of what precedes our action but also what follows it as well.

One can see these ideas at play in Richard's writings on the war. As he writes in "War as the Judgment of God," "For too long a time we have concentrated on human action in international as in other conflicts," while the underlying question of God's action in the war has gone unaddressed.[19] But understanding God as being involved in the war means seeing the war in terms of divine judgment. Richard is at pains to stress, however, that judgment is not only on our enemies, but also on us.

To say that war is God's judgment, Richard argues, means not only that God exacts punishment for our sins but also that God seeks human redemption. God judges in order to redeem, and therefore "war as judgment of God is a purgatory, not a hell."[20] God uses war to chastise, to humble, to convict the nations of their sins in order to draw them back toward God. In this sense, Hitler is the instrument of God to chastise the allies, as much as the allies are God's instruments of judgment against the German people. Through the war, God condemns the pride, the injustice, and the oppression of all parties, particularly insofar as through their warfare they are engaged in acts of crucifixion against the weakest and most vulnerable members of society.

The obligation, then, of Christians in the midst of the war is to respond to God faithfully, refusing to see our enemies as beyond the possibility of redemption while recognizing that God is in the midst of all human actions, even war. War may be carried out, even under the judgment of God, as long as it is carried out in the spirit of contrition and repentance and not for the sake of nation or ideology, but "for the sake of the innocent who must be delivered from the hands of the aggressor."[21]

A further point, which Richard addresses in an essay titled "War as Crucifixion," is the effect of war on the innocent and vulnerable. This fact, which is often lost on the theorists of war who focus on questions of great-power conflict or the formal conformity of nations to legal or theological abstractions, is central to Richard's interpretation of God's presence in the midst of war. Even those who are concerned to ensure that wars be fought morally have to reckon with the fact that, as Richard writes, "in war the burden of suffering does not fall on the guilty, even when the guilt is relatively determinable, but on the innocent."[22] He continues:

> Retribution for the sins of a Nazi party and a Hitler falls on Russian and German soldiers, on the children of Cologne and Coventry, on the Finns and the French. In order that a moral theory may be used it becomes necessary to convict all the common men, the whole opposing nation of guilt. Even if that were possible the theory does not hold since the suffering for guilt is shared by those who are on the side of "justice." Hence those who hold to the moral theory find themselves unable to follow it in practice. If they declare the present war to be just they must participate in the inflicting suffering and death on the "just" with the "unjust"; if they regard the present war as unjust they must stand idly by while the "just" are being made to suffer with the "unjust."[23]

Theology in a World at War

It is this inescapable intertwining of justice and injustice that, for Richard, makes war a kind of crucifixion. It reveals, he argues, "the impossibility of applying the whole scheme of moral judgment and retributive justice to social relations."[24]

The cross yields, he argues, neither to the logic of retributive justice nor to the logic of brute force. It offers a different way of understanding the relationship of God to the world, one that is rooted in God's self-giving love for humanity as demonstrated in Christ's sacrifice on the cross, a sacrifice undertaken not only for the just, but for the unjust as well. In the sight of the cross we must abandon "our moral cynicism along with other peacetime luxuries."[25] The cross "demonstrates the sublime character of real goodness; it is a revelation, though 'in a glass darkly,' of the intense moral earnestness of a God who will not abandon mankind to self-destruction," while at the same time demonstrating "the tragic consequences of moral failure."[26]

To understand war as crucifixion, then, is to realize that the cross, properly understood, forces us to take our moral obligations with greater seriousness, even while it deprives us of easy answers. In the midst of war, we see the meaning of the cross in a different way and are forced to grapple with its significance in our own context, concretely, not in terms of abstractions.

War, understood in light of the cross, is a call to repentance. Repentance is not, Richard stresses, about expressing sorrow for our sins, but is rather "a total revolution of our minds and hearts . . . a great recall from the road of death which we all travel together, the just and the unjust, the victors and the vanquished."[27] War as crucifixion becomes, in this sense, a revelation of God.

Nature and Destiny

"Man has always been his own most vexing problem."[28] So begins Reinhold Niebuhr's *The Nature and Destiny of*

Man, viewed as one of the great contributions to Christian ethics in the twentieth century and Reinhold's magnum opus.[29] Based on his Gifford lectures of 1939, *Nature and Destiny* encapsulates the substance of Reinhold's mature thought and lays the groundwork for his subsequent work through his analysis of the paradoxical nature of the human condition in the world, as creatures of both nature and reason.[30]

Reinhold delivered the lectures in the spring and autumn of 1939. During the second series, his lectures were accompanied by the sounds of anti-aircraft fire in the distance. The reality of the war offered a potent reminder of the importance of Reinhold's central theme of human sin as a reality that pervades all social relations.

In the first volume, *Human Nature*, Reinhold begins with the idea that human beings stand "at the juncture of nature and spirit."[31] We are a problem to ourselves, Reinhold argues, precisely because we misuse our freedom, turning our capacity for self-determination into an attempt to make ourselves the center of our own universe. In doing this, we violate the law of our created nature, which is love, and thus, through sin, contradict the essence of who we are. Modern attempts to understand human nature combine multiple contradictory strands of thought, borrowing and adapting from both Christian and classical conceptions of the self in a way that results in an ultimately confused portrait of the human condition.

The Christian understanding of the human condition, he argues, offers a better account precisely because it recognizes that human beings exist as both natural and rational beings, as beings who are both finite and free. In its freedom, humanity is able to change both the world and its place in it, to become something greater than it is, but in its finitude, humanity finds that it cannot transcend the limits of time and space that are placed on it as a mortal species. Although our imaginations can envision almost limitless possibilities for ourselves, in our lives we are incapable of realizing and accomplishing all of those possibilities. Because of the conflict within human nature between our finitude and freedom, Reinhold argues, sin is inevitable in human life. But it is not *necessary*. There always exists before us the ideal possibility of avoiding sin and remaining suspended within the tension between our finitude and our freedom.

This reality—that we exist as creatures who are both finite and free—is the ground out of which sin grows. While neither finitude nor freedom are themselves sinful, the tension between them produces a state of anxiety within us, which both impels us to creative action in the world and

also tempts us to exceed the boundaries of our finite existence.

Being unable to tolerate our condition of anxiety, human beings seek to resolve the tension by either asserting our will to power in opposition to our finitude or by wallowing in our finitude, "losing ourselves in some nature vitality" instead of engaging responsibly in the ambiguities of the world.[32] The first condition, Reinhold argues, is what Christians understand to be the sin of pride, while the second is the sin of sensuality.

Underlying every manifestation of sin as pride is ultimately an act of deception by which we hide from ourselves and others the reality of our own self-assertion by claiming some higher moral status for our self-seeking, couching our egotism in the language of entitlement, virtue, or merit. But here again is a kind of irony: since we are incapable of acting unjustly toward others without making a moral claim that we are permitted to do so, this is a sort of perverted testimony to our moral status. We need to feel morally justified in our evil, and so we construct elaborate moral justifications for our immorality.

Forms of collective egotism, as on the individual level, are attempts to deny our natural limitations by allowing ourselves to be absorbed into a greater social reality. At the same time, our capacity for injustice and self-righteousness are also magnified to gargantuan size. The larger the group, the more outsize its claims to ultimate power and authority.

Reinhold points out that while sin is a universal human condition, this does not imply that all are equally to blame for the presence of evil and injustice in the world. Thus while there is an "equality of sin" shared by all human beings, there is not an "equality of guilt."[33] It is possible to make judgments and comparisons between more and less just societies and social arrangements, more and less selfish individuals. While it is a mistake to believe that the victims of injustice possess some kind of virtue as a result of their victimhood, the powerful nevertheless possess a greater degree of guilt for historical and social injustice than those who are pushed to the margins by their will to power.

The ideal human possibility is one that stands before God in faith and subjects both its finitude and freedom to the divine will. Doing so, Reinhold insists, is a fulfillment, not the destruction, of our individuality and particularity. It is when we place our center at some point in the universe apart from God, failing to trust in God, that we are subject to the anxiety that compels us to sin. "The sin of inordinate self-love," Reinhold states, thus points to the prior sin of lack of trust in God."[34]

Having described how it is that sin is a problem for humanity, he turns to grace as the solution; but it is not a solution that everyone is looking for. "Nothing is so incredible as the answer to an unasked question," he writes.[35] Whether the Christian answer to the human condition seems credible depends on whether or not one's culture is seeking a Christ. Some cultures seek a Christ; some don't. For those cultures that do not seek a Christ, the Christian message appears to be "foolishness," as St. Paul put it (1 Cor. 1:23 KJV). These cultures do not see history as a realm through which meaning is communicated but seek to escape the fragmentary and partial flux of time and experience, either by absorbing human experience into nature or attempting to fully comprehend it through the exercise of reason.

Divine power cannot be fully disclosed within history, and therefore the sovereignty of God is "hidden," since we cannot ultimately comprehend the mystery of the connection between divine judgment and divine mercy. Hope in a

Theology in a World at War

messiah who will bring the nation to triumph or definitively overcome evil within history are doomed to failure, Reinhold argues. Jesus Christ embodies the fulfillment of the messianic ideal precisely because he disappoints such expectations. While Christ was foolishness to the Greeks because they did not look for fulfillment within history, he became a stumbling block for the Jews because the Christ who was expected did not come in the expected way.

The radical claim made by Christians, Reinhold argues, is that "in the life, death, and resurrection of Christ, the expected disclosure of God's sovereignty over history, and the expected establishment of that sovereignty had taken place."[36] The conflict between Jesus and the Pharisees was rooted in a conflict between a form of legalism that believed that the fulfillment of life could be found within history and a messianism that looked beyond it. The law is ultimately unable to fulfill the claims of Hebraic legalism, Reinhold argues, because a) the law is incapable of fully realizing the reality of human freedom within history, b) it cannot fully take into account the complexity of human motivations, and c) it cannot ultimately restrain evil since the law itself can be made into an instrument of evil.[37]

At the same time, Jesus also rejects the claims of nationalistic messianism. Throughout the New Testament accounts of his ministry, there are examples of Jesus embracing those who fall outside of the realm of those who are deemed to "count" according to rules of nationalistic particularism—whether it be the Syrophoenician woman, the Roman centurion, the woman at the well, or the various disreputable sinners, tax collectors, and prostitutes to whom he preached. The story of the Good Samaritan exemplifies this idea in its most complete form, as does the account of Jesus' temptation in the wilderness.

Jesus' teaching ultimately takes the insights of prophetic tradition to their logical conclusion: if all nations and all peoples are subject to divine judgment, and all human achievements are in some sense compromised by pride and egoism, then the problem raised by the prophets, Reinhold argues, is "not how the righteous will gain victory over the unrighteous, but how the evil in every good and the unrighteousness of the righteous is to be overcome."[38] Jesus' parable of the last judgment symbolizes this reality in its description of the unrighteous who fail to recognize their unrighteousness and the righteous who refuse to accept their own righteousness. "While the righteous are contritely aware of their unworthiness . . . the unrighteous are equally unconscious of their guilt."[39]

Theology in a World at War

If the meaning of history is ultimately understood as a truth that we cannot fully comprehend from within and that can only be revealed within history in the form of suffering love, then, Reinhold argues, the "kingdom of God" that Jesus preaches has a double character: within history, love must remain suffering love, but since love is the law of history itself, it may still have partial and incomplete triumphs within history, since history cannot stand in total contradiction to itself. However, love can never be totally triumphant within history, but always points beyond history to an ultimate revelation beyond history. The "interim" between Jesus' revelation of God's love and justice through his own vicarious suffering and the final triumph of that love beyond history symbolizes the truth that the kingdom of God is pressing upon us within the present moment.[40]

The mistake of the early church was interpreting this symbol literally as a point in the future and failing to recognize that the kingdom is always a possibility here and now, but only in partial form.

In Jesus Christ is manifested the truth of "the ultimate freedom of God above His own law; but not the freedom to abrogate the law."[41] Grace, as Reinhold describes it, is the dual power by which God both completes our incompleteness and overcomes our sin, not through the creation of human moral perfection, but through the manifestation of divine mercy.

The *Nature and Destiny of Man* summed up the stance that would define the nature of Niebuhrian "Christian Realism": a frank attempt to grapple with the reality of human sin and fallibility in the struggle for justice coupled with a fierce moral critique of any form of idealism that refused to see those limitations clearly. Reinhold's rhetorical style, seeking to position the Christian answer as the mean between unacceptable extremes, had a powerfully homiletical effect. He was preaching with the aim of winning converts to a politically and socially engaged Christianity that both refused to turn a blind eye to the problems of evil and injustice in the world and also refused to pretend that there were easy solutions to those problems.

The Children of Light and the Children of Darkness

The Children of Light and the Children of Darkness delves into the relationship between moral idealism and the struggle for social justice. At its heart is Reinhold's much quoted idea that "man's capacity for justice makes democracy possible; but man's inclination to injustice makes democracy necessary."[42] This sentence expresses the central problem of Christian ethics with which Reinhold had been struggling at

Theology in a World at War

least since *Moral Man and Immoral Society*: how to create relative justice in a world of injustice. The moral idealism of the "children of light" would always crash against the rocks of the cynicism of the "children of darkness," who are happy to turn the highest moral aspiration of liberal society to the purpose of pursuing their own narrowly defined self-interest.

Taking his cue from Jesus' admonition to his disciples that "the children of this world are in their generation wiser than the children of light" (Luke 16:8 KJV), Reinhold distinguishes the "moral cynics" from those who, he states, "seek to bring self-interest under the discipline of a moral universal law and in harmony with a more universal good."[43] But the children of light, in their idealism, are ultimately foolish to believe that self-interest can be easily restrained and turned toward the collective good. Their accomplishments are under constant threat by the egoism of the children of darkness, who demonstrate their wisdom because they know the power of self-interest. The children of light, on the other hand, represent genuine virtue because they recognize the validity of a universal idea of the good. They are capable of looking beyond the demands of self-interest and seeing the larger whole, but they are blind to the looming possibility of anarchy, both at home and abroad. Because they labor under a sentimental and superficial understanding of human nature, the children of light do not understand how tenuous the stability of democratic societies can be.

Reinhold aims this critique at both the secular rationalists and the religious liberals who represent the kind of moral sentimentality that he argues is dangerous to the life of a democratic society. What is necessary, he argues, is an understanding of humanity that is neither blinded by sentimentality nor captive to moral cynicism. Reinhold argues: "The children of light must be armed with the wisdom of the children of darkness but remain free from their malice. They must know the power of self-interest in human society without giving it moral justification. They must have this wisdom in order that they may beguile, deflect, harness, and restrain self-interest, individual and collective, for the sake of the community."[44]

The community that Reinhold has in mind is one that is represented by the free and open character of a democratic society. Democracy is *possible* he argues because the children of light rightly understand that human beings are capable of recognizing and acting according to the moral good. Democracy is *necessary*, however, because it prevents the children of darkness from exercising a free hand for the sake of their own self-interest and against the good of the larger community. In an open society, the moral idealism of the children of light can be pitted against the cynicism of the children of darkness and contend in the public sphere for the hearts and minds of the members of the community.

Theology in a World at War

But if the moral idealists insist that their own need for moral purity prevents them from participating in any political enterprise that is less than morally pristine, they leave the field wide open for the children of darkness to triumph, often doing so in the name of the very ideals that the children of light have advocated. Thus, Reinhold insists, it is imperative for moral idealism to be chastened by a realistic account of human nature so that it can both recognize the tendencies to moral cynicism in its own positions and effectively combat the moral cynicism of the children of darkness, whether in the forms of fascism and communism or in the seemingly more benign forms of nationalism and laissez-fair capitalism with which American society was being confronted in the 1940s.

By the war's end, Reinhold had been firmly established as one of the preeminent voices within American Protestantism. His unceasing advocacy of positions that he viewed as being morally important, from the creation of the United Nations and the World Council of Churches to the founding of the State of Israel, put him at the forefront of American religious and political discussion. His appearance on the cover of *Time* magazine in 1948 marked his recognition as the official "establishment theologian."[45] His publication of *Faith and History* in 1949 represented another account of many of the same themes he had addressed throughout the decade. He was regularly invited to take part in State Department conferences on the reconstruction of postwar Europe and other issues of international importance and was eventually invited to membership on the Council on Foreign Relations.[46]

During this same period, ironically, he was also under increased scrutiny by the FBI due to his left-wing affiliations. This was in part because of his increasing involvement with official U.S. policy. FBI agents interviewed many of his friends and family, though they could find no grounds to conclude

The Niebuhr Brothers for Armchair Theologians

that he had any affiliation with the Communist Party. Of course, Reinhold had been as vociferous a critic of communism during the previous two decades as he had been of fascism, though on quite different grounds. None of this prevented him from continuing to take part in the flurry of activity surrounding U.S. postwar policy or in U.S. politics. Although he had eventually come around to a critical support of the New Deal programs of Franklin Roosevelt, he never joined the Democratic Party. Instead he devoted his energies to the local work of the Liberal Party in New York and used his public platform to press for broadly progressive political reforms.[47]

By the end of the 1940s, Reinhold was at the height of his influence and intellectual power. The 1950s would see that influence broaden and in many ways increase, even as Reinhold faced new challenges in both theological and political terms, as well as personally.

CHAPTER FIVE

Revelation and Responsibility

For Richard, the 1940s were a difficult time on a number of fronts. He was shaken by his daughter Cynthia's divorce in the early 1940s, while in 1944 he turned fifty, the same age at which his own father had died.[1] These personal crises, as well as attempts to grapple with the moral meaning of the war, drove him into a deep depression, during which he was hospitalized for a brief period.[2] However, throughout these personal struggles, he continued to reflect deeply on the question of Christian responsibility in the world, enabling him to develop a deeper understanding of the problems of war, nationalism, and democracy for the Christian church.[3]

Richard had been far more ambivalent about the war effort than Reinhold and struggled to find a nuanced way to speak truthfully about the presence of God even in the midst of war and its horrors from within the Christian tradition. In his work throughout the 1940s and 1950s, this careful sense of nuance, of seeking to detect the present action of God in the midst of human affairs, stood at the center of his theology and undergirded much of his publication during this period.

The Meaning of Revelation

The Meaning of Revelation lays out his attempts to deal with the question of revelation in the context of the problem of historical relativism.[4] Here, Richard extends Ernst Troeltsch's study of historicism and seeks to develop an understanding of what it means to come to know about God in the context of the limitations of the human capacity for knowing.[5]

He begins by considering the idea of relativism as the outcome of the modern philosophical realization that "our reason is not only in space-time, but that space-time is in our reason."[6] All human knowledge is knowledge that takes place in the context of particular assumptions about the way that the world works. We do not have direct access to any absolute forms or universal laws, but are rather always historically and socially situated beings "whose metaphysics, logic, ethics, and theology, like their economics, politics, and rhetoric, are limited, moving, and changing in time."[7]

If human knowledge is limited by its historical time and place, then theology as well is subject to a relativistic point of view. There is no standpoint beyond the particularities of the specific Christian community in a specific context from which to examine the truth of theological concepts. Just as philosophy has come up against the limitations that one's perspective places on the capacity to know, so theology also has to reckon with those limitations. We have no knowledge of God, but only of our experience of God within particular times and places.

To acknowledge that human knowledge is relative to time and place does not mean, he argues, that we are trapped in a condition of inward-looking subjectivity. On the contrary, he writes, "It is not apparent that one who knows that his concepts are not universal must also doubt that they are concepts of the universal, or that one who understands how all his experience is historically mediated must believe that nothing is mediated through history."[8] Such a stance insists that, while our knowledge may be subject to time, place, language, and context, it is not exhausted

by those categories. All human knowledge is, in a sense, an act of faith; he argues: "But such faith is inevitable and justifies itself or is justified by its fruits."[9] Christian theology can speak of the God it follows in faith while at the same time recognizing that what it says is limited by its historical context because it believes that God is the source of that faith.

This means, for Richard, that Christian theology is rooted in the life and history of the church: "its home is the church; its language is the language of the church; and with the church it is directed toward the universal from which the church knows itself to derive its being and to which it points all its faith and works."[10] Theology is thus situated in a community and a set of traditions that remain valid for it even as it realizes that these are limitations to its method of inquiry. They are what enable theology to proceed "with confidence in the independent reality of what is seen, though recognizing that its assertions about the reality are meaningful only to those who look upon it from the same standpoint."[11]

By beginning with the historical particularity of the Christian point of view, Richard argues, Christian faith is freed from the need to justify itself according to some other set of criteria and can instead seek to respond faithfully to the revelation of God that they understand in light of that point of view. The God who is revealed from within the Christian point of view is a God who judges us, who challenges our self-aggrandizing attempts to put ourselves, the church, or religion at the center of all things, where only God may stand: "A revelation that can be used to undergird the claim of Christian faith to universal empire over the souls of men must be something else other than the revelation of the God of that Jesus Christ who in faith emptied himself, made himself of no reputation, and refused to claim the kingly crown."[12] These claims are not understandable

Revelation and Responsibility

from a universal perspective, but only make sense from the point of view of the community that trusts itself in faith to following this kind of God.

"Revelation," Richard states, is an "intelligible event which makes all other events intelligible."[13] It is like reading a passage in a book that, once read, illuminates everything else that you've read. It is a special event in the inner life of the community through which that community understands and interprets its entire history. It puts the whole of our lives, the good and the bad, in its proper context and helps us understand how they relate to the narrative of the community's life. In the Christian community, Jesus Christ is the "special occasion," Richard argues, through which the whole of Christian life is understood. This is the sense in which he understands Christ to be the revelation of God.[14] Christ's life and teaching give meaning and pattern to the church's history, enabling it to understand both its triumphs and its tragedies as being related to God's action in the world rather than either a disconnected series of events or as rooted solely in purposeless human drives.

Imagination is a part of all human knowledge, he argues. All attempts to understand the world are rooted in the exercise of our imagination in order to put the world into a comprehensible order. When we discover in reality some dimension that renders it understandable to us, we are using our imaginations to make sense of the world. But this does not mean that we are simply making things up. Reason and imagination cooperate in making the world coherent:

> Reason does not dispense with imagination but seeks to employ apt images and patterns whereby an otherwise inscrutable sensation becomes a true symbol of a reality whose other aspects, as anticipated in the image, are available to common experience. . . . In our external knowledge reason is right imagination; far from ruling out imagination reason depends on its development, so that those most ethereal of poets, the pure mathematicians, become the spies of man's intelligence service and the pioneers of his dominion over nature.[15]

In understanding the world on the basis of revelation, we seek to overcome "the evil imaginations of the heart," those ways of relating to other selves that are destructive and self-serving rather than those that lead us into deeper relationship with others.[16]

Revelation is not the arbitrary decision to interpret our internal history in light of one event rather than another. Rather, revelation compels us to understand our history in a different way. Revelation happens; we do not choose it. It is, Richard states, "the first thing in our community's

Revelation and Responsibility

life, the point from which we proceed and to which we must always go back in thought and deed."[17] But what we proceed from, he argues, is not a core idea or concept. Rather, revelation is the event of encounter with the person of God, and God cannot be analyzed in the way that other objects of our experience are analyzed. We can only come to understand God relationally, as the "Thou" to our "I." We can come to know God only in the context of a relationship through which we are changed in the knowing. We must encounter God as responding selves in relationship to one who knows us more intimately than we know ourselves.

This implies a change in the way we understand ourselves as moral beings. For Christians, morality is not a philosophical, but relational matter; it is grounded in the demand and judgment of God. And transgression of the moral law is not the violation of a principle or the betrayal of a community, but "violence to the body of God" whose son died for our sins.[18] Understood in relationship to the divine will, morality now becomes more radical and all-encompassing, embracing all of humanity and nature within its sphere.

Thus, Richard writes, "Revelation is the beginning of a revolution in our power thinking and our power politics."[19] The same can be said, he argues, of questions of value. Our understanding of what "goodness" means undergoes a transformation in light of God's revelation in Jesus Christ. Whatever natural goods we may value are "transvalued" in the encounter with God in Christ: "The self we loved is not the self God loves, the neighbors we did not prize are his treasures, the truth we ignored is the truth he maintains, the justice which we sought because it was our own is not the justice that his love desires."[20] Through revelation we come to see that the things we thought were valuable in this world are ultimately worthless, while our true good is finally found in refashioning our conception of the good in light of what we come to know of God in Jesus Christ.

Culture and Christianity

In *Christ and Culture,* Richard explores the themes of church and society through the familiar lens of Earnest Troeltsch's sociology. In it, Richard creates a typology through which to compare different approaches to the relationship between Christianity and its social context. His objective is to provide an understanding of the "enduring problem" of how to relate the Christian gospel to the civilization that surrounds it. At some times Christianity seems to be inveterately opposed to its cultural setting; at other times Christianity seems to be deeply assimilated into its surrounding culture.

This problem, Richard argues, is as old as Christianity itself, and Christianity does not, in itself, provide one single answer to the problem, but rather a set of "typical answers" that cover a range of possible relationships between Christianity and culture, none of which wholly encompass the proper relationship between faith and the social order. At times, the relationship seems to be defined by conflict, at others, cooperation. Thus both Christian and non-Christian groups can sometimes be found "calling, for instance, for the elimination of religion from public education, or for the Christian support of apparently anti-Christian political movements."[21]

The first of the five "types" of answers to the question of Christ and culture that Richard considers pits Christ against culture. This type, he notes, emphasizes the fundamental "*opposition* between Christ and culture."[22] The tension between Christ and culture in this model is rooted in the principle that Christ alone wields authority over the life of the Christian. Culture can demand no loyalty from Christians because they recognize in Christ their sole Lord and savior.

The Christ against culture model, exemplified by figures such as Tertullian and Tolstoy, has been important particularly in areas of social reform, whether in the movements for prison reform, the abolitionist movement, or in the struggle to create a just international order. However, Richard is quick to note that "they never achieved these results alone or directly but only through the mediation of believers who gave a different answer to the fundamental question."[23] The Christ against culture model is, he argues, inevitable and necessary, but ultimately inadequate as an approach to Christian ethics.

At the opposite end of the spectrum is the "Christ of culture" model, which Richard associates with the gnostic movements in the early church, with the medieval theology of Peter Abelard, and with the modernism of Albrecht Ritchl. Whereas the Christ against culture model sees in Christ a fundamental rejection of that which is central to culture, the Christ of culture model sees Christ as the fulfillment of all that is best within its culture.

The strength of this model, Richard argues, is in its recognition that Christianity is in a certain sense inescapably cultural. Even fundamentalism is ultimately an expression of a particular brand of cultural loyalty. The Christ of culture model helped facilitate the spread of Christianity in many ways by emphasizing the continuity between Christ and the cultural settings in which Christianity was taking root, and

it placed an emphasis on the universal character of the Christian message. However, the Christ of culture can also become a chameleon, becoming shaped into the image of whatever the cultural context needs him to be: a superman or a sage, a teacher of secret knowledge or of homely virtues. But all of these images, Richard says, are ultimately destroyed by the biblical account of Christ:

> Sooner or later it becomes apparent that the supernatural being was a man of flesh and blood; the mystic a teacher of morals; the moral teacher one who cast out demons by the power of God; the incarnate spirit of love a prophet of wrath; the martyr of a good cause the Risen Lord. It is clear that his commandments are more radical than the Ritschilian reconciliation of his law with the duties of one's calling allows; and that his conception of his mission can never be forced into the pattern of an emancipator from merely human oppressions.[24]

In the end, Richard argues, these two extreme positions, the Christ of and the Christ against culture models, seem to meet one another. They share a number of characteristics in common—suspicion of theology, separation of reason and revelation, and oddly similar accounts of sin, grace, law, and the doctrine of the Trinity.

Richard's three remaining "ideal types" of approach to the problem of Christ and culture exist in some sense "between" these two extreme positions. But he stresses that they aren't "compromise" positions but rather different ways of understanding the nature of the problem. All of these positions recognize that Christ and culture are not simply in opposition to one another, but that Christ and the world are always in some sense related to one another. In the same way, all recognize that God and Christ can't be

opposed to one another; rather, Christians are involved with God-in-Christ and Christ-in-God, and this manifests itself concretely in cultural life.

The Christ above culture model seeks a synthesis between Christ and culture. The synthesis affirms both Christ and culture; it confesses that the Lord is both of this world and of the other. Christ is not simply absorbed by the culture, but he is also not in direct opposition to it. Rather, as Christ is both divine and human, so there is that of the divine and human in culture as well. They can neither be wholly reconciled nor separated. On the other hand, the demands of Christ to turn the other cheek or to give up all one's worldly goods aren't capable of being wholly reconciled with human life in society, but neither can they simply be allegorized, ignored, or projected into the future. As Richard puts it:

> We cannot say "Either Christ or culture," because we are dealing with God in both cases. We must not say, "Both Christ and culture," as though there were no great distinction between them; but we must say, "Both Christ and culture," in full awareness of the dual nature of our law, our end, and our situation.[25]

Richard associates this synthesis approach with the work of the Apologists of the early church as well as with Thomas Aquinas.

Borrowing heavily from the Aristotelian philosophy that was the chief cultural resource of his age, Aquinas offers a Christian theology that is deeply rooted in the use of human reason. Through the use of our reason, we can come to understand God as our ultimate goal. But this entails involvement in both the active and the contemplative life—the life of work and the life of prayer. In our active lives we seek to secure worldly goods for the sake of our temporal happiness, but our ultimate end is beyond the temporal life and with God. Thus human life is always oriented toward both goals, temporal and eternal. And Christians have a responsibility to live their temporal lives in ways that are consistent with their eternal goal, and to guide their societies toward that goal as well.

The irony, Richard states, is that the subsequent "Thomism" of the medieval church destroyed the delicate synthesis that Thomas had constructed. Rather than a theology that used the best of culture to illuminate Christ, particularly as used by Leo XIII, it became another accommodation of Christ to the surrounding culture. Additionally, the synthesis approach too easily seeks to reconcile

God's work with human efforts, and in doing so risks reducing the infinite to the realm of the finite. Finally, Richard says, the synthesist's answer to the question of Christ and culture fails to take account of the depth of sin and radical evil in the human condition.

The next model, which Richard describes as the "dualist" model, sees Christ and culture in paradox with one another. Like the synthesis model, the dualist model also seeks a "both-and" solution, but at the same time, it recognizes the difficulty in resolving the conflict between Christ and culture, and more specifically between the righteousness of God and human righteousness. Sin is the besetting problem for the dualist and therefore it is only the reality of God's grace, rather than any human attribute, that resolves the conflict.

Richard sees this dualist motif most clearly represented in the thinking of the apostle Paul on the one hand and Martin Luther on the other. Paul's writing emphasizes the idea that culture, on its own, does not have the capacity to lead us to Christ. Rather, while social and cultural institutions may hold our worst instincts in check, they cannot show us the way to salvation. Unlike Thomas Aquinas, there are not two different kinds of virtue—moral and theological. Rather the only true virtue to be found is made known through the love of Christ.

This dualist model, Richard argues, has the advantage of being able to account for the dynamic relationship between God and the world in a way that the other models do not. It offers a more realistic assessment of human possibility in the face of God's righteousness and recognizes that not everything that God demands of us in the moral sphere may be easily accomplished within the realm of human experience. The dualist has a better sense of the human condition and offers powerful resources for constructive Christian engagement with the ambiguities of the world.

At the same time, this approach has the disadvantage of encouraging antinomianism on the one hand and cultural conservatism on the other. If all moral decisions are ultimately tainted by sin, this can become an excuse to throw all moral reasoning to the winds. By the same token, if social institutions are viewed primarily as bulwarks against the encroachment of an unconquerable human evil, then it can be tempting to revert to a conservatism that insists that even the most unjust institutions must be left intact for the sake of protecting human society against sin.

In the final model Richard considers is Christ as the transformer of culture. He labels this motif the "conversionist" model. Despite some similarities with the dualist model, this approach begins from a "more positive and hopeful attitude toward culture."[26] The key theological dimension of this approach is an emphasis on God's creative activity in the world through Christ. Human creative work is thus viewed as being a manifestation of God's working in the world, despite the inevitable human tendency to turn such works into acts of self-glorification. This allows for a more affirmative view of the possibilities for human societies to reflect God's will than the dualist viewpoint permits. While sin affects all human accomplishments, this is a reflection of the corruption of a fundamentally good order. God is seen as working in and through history, as human beings respond to the divine call and seek to enact the eschatological hope for the kingdom of God in the midst of human experience.

St. Augustine is the primary exemplar of this model for Richard. "Augustine not only describes, but illustrates in his own person, the work of Christ as converter of culture."[27] His own life and conversion become the model by which the larger conversion of society is understood. "The Roman rhetorician becomes a Christian preacher, who not only puts into the service of Christ the training in language and literature given him by his society, but, by virtue of the freedom and illumination received from the gospel, uses that language with a new brilliance and brings a new liberty to that literary tradition."[28] In the same way, the conversionist model views cultural transformation as taking place through reshaping the best of its culture to the service of Christ.

Even so, this form of conversion does not change the reality of human bondage to sin, even within those individuals or cultures that are in the process of transformation. Evil remains the besetting problem at the heart of the human condition. The conversionist position recognizes that this is an issue not just on the individual level but also on the social level, as all human cultural achievements labor to rise above its tendency to depravity:

Friendship is corrupted by treachery; the home, "natural refuge from the ills of life," is itself not safe; the political order in city and empire is not only confused by wars and oppressions, but the very administration of justice becomes a perverse business in which ignorance seeking to check vice commits new injustice. Disorder extends to every phase of culture; diversity of language and efforts to impose a common language, just wars as well as unjust, efforts to achieve peace and to establish dominion, the injustice of slavery and the requirement that men act justly as masters of slaves in the midst of this injustice—all these and many other aspects of social existence are symptoms of man's corruption and misery.[29]

And yet, even here, sin is never triumphant. God overcomes and redeems human sin even at its most perverse, on both the individual and societal levels. Both individually and corporately, God has the last word against sin.

In the concluding chapter of *Christ and Culture*, Richard argues that there is no definitive and exclusive model of Christ's relationship to culture that can be embraced to the exclusion of all others. Each model offers something valuable to the Christian understanding of how the church should relate to the world in the midst of which it dwells. Individuals and communities of faith must take on the responsibility of answering for themselves how Christ and culture intersect, or if they do at all. This decision, Richard argues, must be made in the knowledge that all of our knowledge and action takes place in a partial and fragmentary way, and yet must be made in faith:

> To make our decisions in faith is to make them in view of the fact that no single man or group or historical time is the church; but that there is a church of faith in which we do our partial, relative work and on which we count. It is to make them in view of the fact that Christ is risen from the dead, and is not only the head of the church but the redeemer of the world. It is to make them in view of the fact that the world of culture—man's achievement—exists within the world of grace—God's kingdom.[30]

The Center of Value

Richard begins *Radical Monotheism and Western Culture* by considering the way in which theology as a mode of study is distinct from other disciplines, such as geology or anthropology. Unlike those disciplines, we can only come to know the *object* of our inquiry (God) through our *subjective* act of faith. The two are inextricably linked: God cannot be studied without reference to faith in God. While in the nineteenth century theologians were often tempted to reduce theology wholly to the subjective dimension of faith, Richard argues "the subjective can no more be meaningfully abstracted from the objective than vice versa."[31] If we can't study God without faith, we also can't study faith without God: "Hence when we carry on theological work we must do so as men who participate in faith, who exercise faith even while they are criticizing it, who are reflective about faith in their reflections on God, the object of faith."[32]

At the same time, he argues, faith is not in opposition to reason, but rather theology reasons *from* faith and *in* faith. Thus faith is not the conclusion of a process of rational analysis, but rather the starting point from which the theologian seeks to understand what it is in which he or she has

faith. To do this, the theologian must first learn to reason about the faith he or she possesses as well as learn to engage in a responsible critique of that faith. Just as the literary critic cannot fruitfully engage in criticism without knowing something of literature, so the theologian can only critique the life of faith from within.

From this perspective, Richard argues, faith has a double character, both as trust and as fidelity. As trust, faith is an expression of confidence in the truth and worth of that which one values; however, as loyalty, it is a willingness to act and live on behalf of that which one values. This concept of faith doesn't apply only to God, but to any potential center of value, such as friendship or nation. When our gods fail, when those things that we value prove not to be the centers of value that we believed them to be, then faith is betrayed, but the desire for faith, he argues, may be a universal human trait, even when that god may be something other than the transcendent God of the Christian faith.

A god, Richard explains, needn't refer to a supernatural being. Rather, he argues, the word "god" is better understood as referring to a value-center or a cause. In this sense, the modern alternatives are not only between belief in a transcendent being or atheism, but rather the myriad possible centers of value from which humans may pick. There is no one who can be truly said to be an atheist, since we all operate out of a center of value.

In this sense, Richard argues, we are often either henotheists, motivated primarily by one center of value among many, or polytheists, attempting to follow many centers of value simultaneously. In either case, the god we worship represents a center of value or centers of value to which we devote our faith without necessarily attributing to it any kind of supernatural character.

Revelation and Responsibility

Modern nationalism powerfully and troublingly illustrates the character of henotheistic, or social faith. Richard argues:

> Nationalism shows its character as a faith whenever national welfare or survival is regarded as the supreme end of life; whenever right and wrong are made dependent on the sovereign will of the nation, however determined; whenever religion and science, education and art, are valued by the measure of their contribution to the national existence, by these tests nationalist faith shows its pervasive presents to us in our common life every day in schools and churches no less than in political utterances and policies.[33]

Nationalism is hardly the only place where henotheism can be found in modern society. Marxism follows many of the same tropes as nationalism in its version of social faith. And even purportedly monotheistic faiths can often, in practice, become henotheistic.

While henotheism at least offers a relative unity of life by rooting our center of value within the society or social group, polytheism, as Richard describes it, embraces a pluralism of centers of value. When there is no single center of value in which to place one's faith, he argues, human loyalties are scattered to multiple causes. "When the half-gods go the minimal gods arrive."[34] Richard sees Epicureanism and existentialism as responses to the dissolution of social faith that seek to substitute the self for the lack of a unified center of value. These faiths "look like ghostly survivals of faith among men who, forsaken by the gods, continue to hold on to life."[35]

Radical monotheism by contrast seeks its center of value not in the closed society or the myriad competing centers of

The Niebuhr Brothers for Armchair Theologians

value that impinge upon us. Rather "its reference is to no one reality among the many but to One beyond all the many, whence all the many derive their being, and by participation in which they all exist. As faith, it is reliance on the source of all being for the significance of the self and all that exists."[36] Radical monotheism roots its faith not in some being or beings among other beings, but in the principle of Being itself.

Radical monotheism identifies the principle of being and the principle of value as being one and the same. As faith, it takes the identity of these as its starting point. The principle of being encompasses and values all that exists and demands loyalty toward all that exists while at the same time recognizing that being itself transcends all actually existing things. This is the basis of the love commandment in

Christianity. While every faith, he argues, demands the love of one's neighbor, by circumscribing the center of value around some finite thing or things, it also excludes from its circle some portion of the world as being the enemy:

> Love of the neighbor is required in every morality formed by a faith; but in polytheistic faith the neighbor is defined as the one who is near me in my interest group, *when* he is near me in that passing association. In henotheistic social faith my neighbor is my fellow in the closed society. Hence in both instances the counterpart of the law of neighbor-love is the requirement to hate the enemy. But in radical monotheism my neighbor is my companion in being; though he is my enemy in some less than universal context the requirement is to love him. To give to everyone his due is required in every context; but what is due to him depends on the relation in which he is known to stand.[37]

Moral principles, Richard argues, find their most universal expression through radical monotheism, even when they are interpreted in ways that conform more to norms of social religion or polytheism.

Radical monotheism, he continues, differs from other, similar faiths by virtue of its universal character. Even such encompassing faiths as humanism or naturalism, he argues, are ultimately restatements of the basic social faith of henotheism, but taking as their center of value humanity or the natural world. Each of these faiths rests on some form of closed society, from which the rest of existence is excluded. Radical monotheism, by contrast, is genuinely *all encompassing*. "Radical monotheism," he states, "dethrones all absolutes short of the principle of being itself. At the same time, it reverences every relative existent. Its two great

mottos are: 'I am the Lord thy God; though shalt have no other gods before me' and 'Whatever is, is good.'"[38]

We come to understand the incarnation of radically monotheistic faith as it is disclosed to us in revelation. Paradigmatically this is seen in the revelation of God to Moses on Sinai, when God declares "I am who I am" through which, Richard states, it is revealed both that God is being itself and that being itself is God, both valuer and savior, and Moses is challenged to accept faith in this radically monotheistic God as the center of his value. In the same vein, the Christian expression of faith in Jesus Christ as savior strikes these notes as well:

> When Christians refer to Jesus Christ as the revelation of God they do not or ought not have less than

the three notes of faith in mind, the note of the valuing saving power in the world is the principle of being itself; that the ultimate principle of being gives and maintains and re-establishes worth; that they have been called upon to make the cause of that God their cause. It is of course a fact that Christians, like Jews, often have other things in mind when they speak of revelation. . . . Yet insofar as the Christ event elicits radical faith it is seen as demonstration of Being's loyalty to all beings and as call to decisive choice in God's universal cause.[39]

At the same time that revelation discloses the radically monotheistic character of being, it also discloses the personal character of faith in being. For faith to be understood as both trust and loyalty, it has to be understood in the first person: "To say that God makes himself known as First Person is to say that revelation means less the disclosure of the essence of objective being to minds than the demonstration to selves of faithful, truthful being."[40]

Radical monotheism, by contrast, cannot be limited to a particular set of symbols or doctrines, but rather overflows any particular belief system, recognizing them all as partial or limited expressions of the Holy itself. Radical monotheism thus at the same time secularizes the experience of the holy while sanctifying all of existence:

> When the principle of being is God—i.e., the object of trust and loyalty—then he alone is holy and ultimate sacredness must be denied to any special being. No special places, times, persons, or communities are more representative of the one than any others are. No sacred groves or temples, no hallowed kings or priests, no festival days, no chosen communities are particularly representative of Him in whom all things

live and move and have their being. A Puritan iconoclasm has ever accompanied the rise of radical faith.[41]

Just as radical monotheism takes as its motto that whatever is, is good, so it recognizes that every being is holy. Yet religion often thrives precisely on separating the sacred from the secular, the holy from the profane. The temptation toward social religion always lurks within the heart of monotheistic faith, as human beings always seek to circumscribe the realm of faith so as to exclude the unworthy.

In the end, the heart of radical monotheism is to be found in its commitment to the principle of being itself, which transcends the particularities of all of its various expressions. Only through such a commitment can radical monotheism be separated from the social and pluralistic faiths that at every turn attempt to transform the universal into an expression of the particular. As Richard notes in

closing: "A radically monotheistic faith says to them as to all other claimants to 'the truth, the whole truth, and nothing but the truth,' to all the 'circumnavigators of being' as [George] Santayana calls them: 'I do not believe you. God is great.'"[42]

The Responsible Self

At the time of his death, Richard had been working on a book that would offer an integral presentation of his own approach to ethics, which he had taught for many years at Yale as "The Structure and Dynamics of the Moral Life."[43] After he died, it was published under the title *The Responsible Self*. In this volume, Richard lays out a method of Christian moral thought and a phenomenology of human moral existence.

Richard begins by explaining that the book is more of an exercise in Christian moral philosophy than theology because while it is "Bible-informed" it is not "Bible-centered."[44] He is writing, he argues "as a Christian who is seeking to understand the mode of his existence and that of his fellow beings as human agents."[45] Harkening back to some of the themes of *Radical Monotheism and Western Culture*, he explains his understanding of the Christian faith as being rooted in his self-identification as a follower of Christ ("though I travel at a great distance from him" he notes) and as one who identifies with the cause of Christ "who lived and died and rose again for his cause of bringing God to men and men to God and so also of reconciling men to each other and the world."[46] Rooting his analysis in the radically monotheistic position he had outlined in his earlier work, he aims to move toward an examination of Christian ethics from within the Christian point of view rather than on the basis of some external perspective.

The word "responsibility," Richard argues, is the core concept of ethical action. To be responsible means being *capable of responding* to the claims that are put on us through our actions. We may also understand ourselves through other moral categories, such as that of the Maker or the Lawgiver, the capacity to "answer," to respond, is central to our moral identity. It exists alongside and informs the image of us as both makers and law-givers:

> When the word, responsibility, is used of the self as agent, as doer, it is usually translated with the aid of the older images as meaning direction toward goals or as ability to be moved by respect for law. Yet the understanding of ourselves as responsive beings, who in all our actions answer to action upon us in accordance with our interpretation of such action, is a fruitful conception, which brings into view aspects of our self-defining conduct that are obscured when the older images are exclusively used.[47]

Thus, Richard argues, while an ethics that understands human beings first and foremost as makers asks about what our end or goal is, and an ethics that understands us first as citizens and law-givers asks first about the law that governs human action, an ethic of responsibility asks a different question. "Responsibility," he argues, "proceeds in every moment of decision and choice to inquire, 'What's going on?'"[48]

As responding creatures, we interpret our situation and respond to actions upon us. But we are also accountable for the consequences of our actions and need to be aware of the reactions that our own acts are likely to produce in others. What's more, responsibility requires that we consider our actions within the total social context of which we are a part. We act neither as isolated individuals nor within

Revelation and Responsibility

small groups, but within the larger social whole to which we belong.

Moral action is divided up between considerations of the *good*, the *right*, and the *fitting*. An ethic rooted in responsibility, he writes, is one that through its interpretation of the total situation is capable of determining the true nature of the right and the good.

As social beings, we are selves in the presence of other selves. That is to say, a fundamental dimension of what it means to be human is to be related and associated with other human beings. We do not experience ourselves first as isolated individuals but always as selves in the midst of other selves, as related to "the face-to-face community in which unlimited commitments are the rule and in which every aspect of every self's existence is conditioned by membership in the interpersonal group."[49] Thus we always understand our actions, and react to others' actions upon us, in this relational way.

Additionally, as selves, we have the capacity to step outside of ourselves, view ourselves as an "impartial spectator" and judge our own actions. And we also respond to the actions of others in the context of the larger pattern of relationship in which we are involved. When we speak of conscience, Richard argues, we are describing our capacity as selves to respond in awareness of the whole set of interpersonal relationships of which we are a part. We are always in dialogical relationships with ourselves, the natural world, and the transcendent dimension of reality. Thus, Richard argues, in the experience of the monotheistic believer, "the responsible self is driven as it were by the movement of the social process to respond to and be accountable in nothing less than a universal community."[50]

Our selves also exist in an even larger context, as beings who exist in "absolute dependence" upon a larger reality, not only than ourselves, but also than any of the finite relationships in which we find ourselves. In other words, as selves we experience our existence as dependent upon an infinite source—God. We come to understand our absolute dependence upon God as "the radical action whereby we are ourselves in the here and now."[51]

There are many ways to interpret the fact of our absolute dependence, though within the Christian tradition it is finally understood through the lens of faith, which Richard describes as entailing both the possibility of trust and mistrust in God. It is not a given that we must relate to God in trust. Our response to the reality of our absolute dependence on God is deeply personal and can just as easily manifest itself in mistrust. But in either case is an act of faith.

As responsible selves, responding to God in either trust or mistrust, we are faced with the possibility of putting our loyalty in some cause or another that is less than God. If we do so, we may place our center of value in our selves, or

Revelation and Responsibility

nations, or the good of science or humanity, but these will always be finite causes. On the other hand, it is always possible for us to respond to God in trust, placing our center of value in being itself.

As responsible selves, we are in conflict with the multiple forces that act upon us and toward which we are required to respond, and we are in conflict with ourselves and the multiple drives and potential responses that we may give to our situation. We can flee from responsibility by acting only for ourselves and for the insular societies or ideologies to which we belong or adhere. Viewing God as an enemy, we nevertheless experience God as present to us as the one who is present in our every action, even in our sin. Yet this way of seeing God as the enemy is, Richard argues, the body of death, through which we experience our own wretchedness and despair.

Salvation in this case comes to us through a turning away from this fear of God as the enemy and toward the experience of God in trust that all that exists, including death, ultimately exists for the sake of renewal and life. And this trust is embodied for Christians in the life, death, and resurrection of Jesus Christ. Through the symbol of the resurrection we come to understand ourselves as reconciled with one another and with God, and thus to turn away from our view of God as the enemy and interpret our situation in response to the faith elicited by Jesus Christ, which points to the healing and forgiveness of all things.

CHAPTER SIX

To Accept What We Cannot Change

In the postwar years, Reinhold's reputation had reached its apex. He appeared on the cover of *Time* magazine, worked as a consultant for the state department, was inducted as a member of the Council on Foreign Relations, and continued his nonstop schedule of lecturing, preaching, and writing. By the beginnings of the 1950s, he was well established as the leading liberal protestant public intellectual in the United States. His outspoken opposition to communism and his frequently incisive commentary on U.S. foreign policy added to his stature as *the* theologian of the establishment.

At the same time, however, Reinhold was not willing to simply parrot the establishment line on issues such as the creation of the hydrogen bomb, about which he wrote, "Thus we have come into the tragic position of developing a form of destruction which, if used by our enemies against us, would mean our physical annihilation; and if used by us against our enemies, would mean our moral annihilation."[1] In the end, he supported the creation of the hydrogen bomb, but only as a deterrent against the Soviet Union.[2] He also supported the execution of the Rosenbergs[3] but was adamantly opposed to the excesses of the McCarthy hearings, even as he worked to persuade his friends and acquaintances to avoid contact with organizations that were suspected of communist affiliations.[4]

None of this prevented him from once again becoming the target of an FBI investigation. The Red Scare was in full bloom by the early 1950s, in the wake of the communist takeover of China and the development of the Soviet atom bomb. While the McCarthy hearings were the most visible manifestation of America's rising anticommunist panic, there were other signs. Reinhold was regularly singled out

as a potential communist by loyalist groups, along with other liberal Christian colleagues.[5] The FBI continued to keep tabs on Reinhold throughout the 1950s and into the 1960s, without ever finding anything more than innuendo and suspicion to hang on him. Reinhold's general affiliation with the political left, and his participation in the Socialist and Liberal parties, came under scrutiny, as did his support for the antifascist forces during the Spanish Civil War, while little attention was paid to his frequent, public, and vociferous denunciations of communism.[6] His FBI file also noted that Reinhold taught a course at Union Theological Seminary titled "Christianity and Communism" without ever noting that the theme of the course was the contrast between the two.[7]

The Irony of American History

In 1952, Reinhold offered his reflections on the moral possibilities and risks of the Cold War era in *The Irony of American History*.[8] Irony, he argues, differs from both pathos and tragedy in that, whereas pathos describes situations of suffering for which the sufferer is not responsible and tragedy describes situations in which evil acts are done for the sake of some larger good, "irony consists of apparently fortuitous incongruities in life which are discovered, upon closer examination, to be not merely fortuitous." He goes on to explain:

> A comic situation is proved to be an ironic one if a hidden relation is discovered in the incongruity. If virtue becomes vice through some hidden defect in the virtue; if strength becomes weakness because of the vanity to which strength may prompt the mighty man or nation; if security is transmuted into insecurity because too much reliance is placed upon it; if

wisdom becomes folly because it does not know its own limits—in all such cases the situation is ironic.[9]

Reinhold was acutely aware of the incongruities that were emerging in the American confrontation with the Soviet Union, how easily our virtues could turn to vices, strengths to weaknesses, and security to insecurity. The book was written in a tone of stern warning to the United States that an excessive belief in its own righteousness could backfire in unanticipated ways.

The Irony of American History applies many of the themes that Niebuhr had developed in the thirties and forties to the new situation. He had already established the idea that group egoism and self-justification led nations to believe too strongly in their own nobility in *Moral Man and Immoral Society*, while in *The Nature and Destiny of Man* he had written of the innate limitations on all human knowledge and power. In *Beyond Tragedy* he had grappled with the way in which dramatic tropes could illuminate the human condition, and throughout the late 1930s and the 1940s he had applied these lessons to American involvement in Europe.

The irony of America's situation in the cold war era for Niebuhr is the recognition that its strength comes from the central belief in its status as an "innocent" nation. The idea of "American exceptionalism" is based on this idea, that as a nation we were born without the taint that infects the history of other nations. This idea, which finds expression in both the Puritan rhetorical of the "city on a hill" and the Jeffersonian belief in our innate virtue as a nation, leads to the belief that as a nation we are set apart from the rest:

> Whether our nation interprets its spiritual heritage through Massachusetts or Virginia, we came into

existence with the sense of being a "separated" nation, which God was using to make a new beginning for mankind. We had renounced the evils of European feudalism. We had escaped from the evils of European religious bigotry. We had found broad spaces for the satisfaction of human desires in place of the crowded Europe. Whether, as in the case of the New England theocrats, our forefathers thought of our "experiment" as primarily the creation of a new and purer church, or as in the case of Jefferson and his coterie, they thought primarily of the new political community, they believed in either case that we had been called out by God to create a new humanity.[10]

But of course, American history is filled with refutations of the idea of our original innocence. Slavery, colonialism, the genocide of Native Americans, all testify to the

self-deception that lay underneath the myth of American innocence. And yet, Niebuhr declares, "we could not be virtuous (in the sense of practicing the virtues which are implicit in meeting our vast world responsibilities) if we were really as innocent as we pretend to be."[11]

In our self-deception, we are actually enabled, he argues, to act as we must in the midst of the current situation. In our belief that we don't really desire global power, we become capable of exercising it responsibly, particularly with regard to the threat of nuclear war. A truly innocent nation could never possess a nuclear weapon. Yet a nation that believes itself falsely to be innocent could possess one as a deterrent, but be moved by its own self-deceptive confidence in its innocence never to use it, lest we "cover ourselves with a terrible guilt."[12] Thus the ironic situation of a powerful America that claims to be uninterested in power wielding a weapon of ultimate destruction that it can neither morally renounce nor morally use underscores the ambiguity of warfare. It also accentuates the ambiguity of the American role on the global stage.

Communism has its own version of this illusion of original innocence, Reinhold argues, which is more pernicious because it is more consistently held. Whereas liberalism supports its illusions through a general dogma that human beings can be improved through better education, communism thrusts the blame for evil onto capitalism as an institution. The abolition of capitalism is thus the reestablishment of the condition of original innocence. Thus, for communism the elimination of capitalism becomes the justification for all kinds of "monstrous evils" done from the presumption of its own innocence.[13] By contrast America is saved, Reinhold argues, from being wholly insufferable by the fact that we insist on our innocence less consistently than the communists insist on theirs and allow for the expression of dissenting ideas in the public realm, which allows for a more realistic assessment of our role in the world.

Both Marxism and liberalism also labor under the illusion that human societies are capable of becoming the masters of their own destiny. This manifests itself in competing brands of political messianism. Yet ultimately our desire for self-mastery leads us to desire greater security for ourselves. This leads us more and more deeply into involvement in global affairs and to leadership within the coalition of nations arrayed in opposition to communism. Yet here Reinhold encounters another irony: in acquiring immense global power we have taken on a responsibility for the world that limits our freedom to exercise that power. As he says, "a strong America is less completely master of its own destiny than was a comparatively weak America, rocking in the cradle of its continental security and serene in its infant innocence."[14]

The illusion of self-mastery lies beneath many of the ironies Reinhold saw America confronting in the midst of the cold war. Our desire for happiness leads us to material prosperity and comfort but ultimately reveals the limits of our ability to achieve happiness through material comfort. Our global power simply reveals to us how limited our power ultimately is, while our confidence in our own virtue leads us into vice. Our desire to control our world through the exercise of our reason ultimately shows us only that many of the most powerful forces in history and society are not susceptible to "rational" control.

The central flaw, Reinhold argues, in both the Marxist and Liberal illusions about history is their reliance on ideologies that are immune to actual experience. Both take partial truths about human life and society and harden them into immutable and exclusive truths while failing to recognize their own limitations. The ideological struggle

The Niebuhr Brothers for Armchair Theologians

prevents them from pragmatically addressing their ideological limitations and seeking to ground their social policy in experience. The postwar American and European political experiments in a mixed economy and welfare state allowed both societies to achieve a measure of social justice that refuted the Marxist claims that government exists only to serve the interests of the ruling classes.

While these social experiments demonstrate, as Reinhold has it, the triumph of experience over dogma, this is not to say that these societies don't have their own limitations. In the case of the United States in particular, Reinhold notes that we have our own ideological blind spots rooted in our failure to account for private property as an instrument of power, which can be used for private gain but can also be used for social justice and in our failure to recognize the instabilities associated with a free enterprise economy. America's great advantage over the Soviet Union in sorting through these ideological and pragmatic considerations is its democratic character.

In the final analysis, Reinhold argues, only humility in the face of the vast forces of history can allow us to overcome the ironies of our situation. The struggle for mastery and the desire to control those historical forces are what lead us into the contradictions that appear so ironic when viewed clearly. Thus the lesson of *The Irony of American History* is how little is really within human control and how necessary it is to look beyond the immediate situation to take in the larger historical context in which we live.

Self, Society, and History

In early 1952, Reinhold suffered a series of strokes that seriously limited his ability to write or participate with his usual fervor in public events.[15] Although unable to be fully engaged, he continued to wield influence where he could, aiding Adlai Stevenson in the 1952 elections to the extent that he was able, but largely rendered passive by his illness.

By 1953, he had recovered sufficiently to produce a volume entitled *Christian Realism and Political Problems*, which is particularly notable for the essay "Augustine's Political Realism."[16] In this essay, Reinhold ties his own brand of Christian realism to the realism evident in Augustine's *City of God*. The distinction, Reinhold argues, between the *civitas terrena* and the *civitas dei* represents the essential tension within Christian realist arguments. The condition of the worldly city demands an account of sin, self-interest, and deception in all human societies and relationships. But faith in the city of God denies us easy recourse to nihilism or cynicism since it represents the possibility of overcoming the illusions of the worldly city through the manifestation of the perfect love of God. In a sense, this essay encapsulates a quip that Reinhold once made to Will Scarlett, regarding comparisons between Karl Barth and Paul Tillich, and Tertullian and Origen, respectively: "About Barth and Tillich and myself. I wouldn't want to be Tertullian. He was too obscurantist. I would rather emulate Augustine."[17]

In 1955 he published *The Self and the Dramas of History*, through which he criticized Freudian psychology and the psychoanalytic movement.[18] Building on some themes he initially developed in *The Nature and Destiny of Man*, he elaborates further on the idea of the human self as a unique entity that engages in freedom in constant dialogue with

itself, with others, and with God. This dialogue is manifested through the drama of history, through which the self comes to find meaning. The biblical account of faith, he argues, ultimately provides better resources for providing meaning to the self and establishing a moral basis for community and social cohesion than the options provided by forms of modern rationalism and psychoanalysis.

Reinhold's next volume, *Pious and Secular America*, was published in 1958.[19] During this period he continued to struggle with the aftereffects of his stroke, as well as a bout of depression and political discouragement in the face of Eisenhower's reelection.[20] At the same time, he witnessed with mounting concern the rise of Billy Graham's form of pietistic revivalism, which seemed to him to lure Christians away from a commitment to the struggle for justice within society and made the Christian message too shallow and easy to accept. Graham's Christ was, as his brother might have said, a "Christ of culture" in need of a greater degree of cultural criticism.[21]

Reinhold's critique of the complacency and pietism of the Eisenhower era stand at the center of *Pious and Secular America*. The collection of nine essays explores how the United States is capable of being at the same time both a strongly religious yet emphatically secular nation. Paradoxically, he argues, both the religious and secular characters of American life depend on one another. They interpenetrate one another, he argues, "by the effect of definitely ascertainable historic causes peculiar to the American experience."[22] Frontier religion brought together the sectarian pietism of Baptist and Methodist faith with a social pragmatism that reimagined religion less and less in terms of questions of "eternal reward" and more and more in terms of practical questions of economics and political life. "Thus," Reinhold writes, "the Enlightenment and evangelical Christianity were merged on the American frontier and the result was that note of sentimentality which has characterized both political and religious thought in the nation ever since."[23]

Billy Graham in many ways exemplifies the self-satisfaction of mid-century Christian faith, Reinhold argues. Graham brings the simplistic pietism of frontier Christianity into the modern age, ensuring believers of their own righteousness and ignoring the persistence of sin and the intractable problems of social justice. Graham's evangelism, he states, "has a blandness which befits the Eisenhower era. The miracle is accomplished by signing a decision card while the choir sings softly."[24]

To Accept What We Cannot Change

In the end, both easy pietism and self-satisfied secularism give testimony to the flabbiness of Christianity in the Eisenhower era. Both evade the mystery and challenge of traditional Christian faith, which "presents the beauty and terror of life without evasion,"[25] and which reveals in the symbol of the suffering and crucified messiah the powerful truth of a loving and merciful God who is both our origin and our end.

In 1959, Reinhold published *The Structure of Nations and Empires*, which represented the third volume of a loose trilogy of books published after his stroke.[26] While *The Self and the Dramas of History* was focused on the human person within the broad sweep of historical meaning, and *Pious and Secular America* was focused on the malaise of religion and society in Eisenhower's America, *The Structure of Nations and Empires* sought to offer a broad philosophy of history and a theory of international relations. Unlike many of his other writings, here he relies very little on theological or ethical insights rooted in his understanding of the Christian faith. This volume, more than most of his writings, is a pure exposition of political philosophy.

Picking up on some of the themes from *The Irony of American History*, particularly having to do with the dynamics of the cold war conflict between the United States and the Soviet Union, *The Structure of Nations and Empires* seeks to place that conflict into the context of the historical development of empires throughout history, examining the dynamics that underlie the formation of all societies. All communities, he argues, rely on both internal forces of cohesion and some form of central authority to tie society's disparate interests together with one another. Societies are traditionally organized around the need for some form of order, but the demands for justice and equality can stand in tension with the need for order, and modern democratic states seek to provide a balance between the need for proximate justice and the need for the maintenance of some kind of social order and cohesion.

Empires are defined centrally by their use of power to expand their territory and influence. Imperial power tends to be wielded through the vertical power of some form of central authority, in the form of some sovereign power that stands for the cohesive unity of the empire. Reinhold analyzes this dynamic using the Roman and Chinese empires as case studies in imperial structure and then turns to consider the way in which Christianity both formed and was formed by this encounter with the Roman empire.

America is constrained by the fact that, on the one hand, it stands as one among many autonomous nation-states in

the modern world, yet it wields unprecedented unilateral power, both in terms of its economic power and its nuclear arsenal. However, Reinhold argues, the United States has no genuine desire to be an empire or act imperially in the world. This is one of the ironies of American history that he had noted in his earlier work. Yet it finds itself in conflict with a genuine imperial power in the Soviet Union. As a result, the United States has no choice but to exercise its power in an imperial way while at the same time seeking to avoid becoming an empire in fact. Institutions designed to create conditions of "collective security" can aid in some respects, but ultimately even the United Nations cannot create the ideological and political unity necessary to bring the conflicts of nations and empires to an end. Finally, Reinhold argues, the problems of international relations are beyond the capacity of any set of individuals or moment in time to solve. "Only," he states, "a religious faith and a humanism more profound than the many extant varieties can make sense out of these terrifying facts of modern history, particularly those facts which prove that all historic responsibilities must be borne without the certainty that meeting them will lead to any ultimate solution to the problem."[27]

The View From the Sidelines

After retiring from Union Theological Seminary in 1959, Reinhold spent a term lecturing at Harvard, but by the early 1960s he had given up most of his touring and lecturing activities. His health made writing increasingly difficult for him, and he spent most of his time at his house in Heath, Massachusetts. He nevertheless kept a close eye on political developments on both the domestic and international scenes, and he continued to be involved to the extent that he could. He wrote frequently for a wide array of publications, including *The Christian Century* and *Christianity and Crisis*. Additionally, he was able to produce three final volumes of reflections on religion, society, and political life in the last decade of his life, of which *Man's Nature and His Communities* is the most significant. He also managed to draw the attention of the FBI one final time.

Man's Nature and His Communities, written in 1965, offers an important perspective on the evolution of Reinhold's thought. In it he offers his equivalent of St. Augustine's *Retractiones*, rethinkings and revisions of ideas that he had developed in earlier works.[28] While a slim volume, in it Reinhold attempts to clarify and modify concepts that had been central to his thought from early on.

The bulk of *Man's Nature and His Communities* is an attempt to rethink the significance of his approach to "realism" as a way of conceiving of Christian responsibility within society. The most important revision in his approach is his move away from the largely theological language and framework of *The Nature and Destiny of Man* and toward a more philosophically neutral analysis of the history of political thought.[29]

The central essay revisits the tension between realist and idealist political theories within Western thought. Reinhold defines the tension between the two positions thusly:

> Realists emphasize the disruptive effect of human freedom on the community . . . the idealists, on the other hand, regard man's freedom primarily in terms of its creative capacity to extend the limits of man's social sense and to bring order out of the confusion of his impulses and out of the chaos of his conflicting social ambitions, and to give preference to his "moral" or social sense over his self-regard.[30]

To Accept What We Cannot Change

Human freedom is rooted in our existence as both social and rational creatures. As social creatures, we are integrated into webs of relationships rooted ultimately in natural impulses. But as rational creatures, we recognize our freedom to break those bonds and define ourselves. The idealism is rooted in the expectation that we will use our expanding conception of our own freedom to tighten the bonds of sociality within human communities. Realists, on the other hand, recognize that, while that may and often does happen, it is by no means guaranteed. Human freedom can destroy as much as, if not more than, it creates community.

As he traces this thread from Aristotle, through Hobbes and Locke, to Marx and Freud, he develops his argument that the Christian faith, in its recognition that self-regarding and social impulses are at war with one another in human nature and that self-regard usually gets the upper hand. He also offers an inherently realistic assessment of the human condition while at the same time not granting to Christians any necessarily better idea of what to do about the problem of human conflict than anyone else.

Regardless of our ideals we must contend with the tension between the universal values that we possess as humans and the narrow and parochial interests we inherit as members of nations, races, and tribes of various sorts. The tribalism that results in inhumanity and barbarism manifests itself both in overt wars between communities and in the oppression of weaker peoples by those who are stronger.

But the paradox of human society, Reinhold argues, is that on the one hand, the evidence on behalf of the existence of universal human values is increasingly validated through the social sciences, while on the other any sober assessment of human history will attest to the ready abandonment of those values in the face of tribal loyalties. Whether it is the oppression of racial or ethnic minorities on the basis of skin color or language or of religious minorities on the basis of beliefs, human beings possess a strong penchant for drawing lines of demarcation between "us" and "them," particularly when they can secure or promote their own power and influence by doing so.

The ultimate irony of the human condition, both individually and socially, is in the end that the constant desire to secure one's own self-interests is ultimately self-defeating. Only by engaging in acts of self-giving, acting for the sake of another, can human beings gain the security and freedom they desire. "Thus we have a complete circle of the paradox: consistent self-seeking is self-defeating; but self-giving is impossible without resources furnished by the community, in the first instance, the family."[31] It is ultimately the law of love, rather than any narrow or parochial concern, that can lead us out of tribalism and toward universal community. But this law of love cannot be obeyed without the aid of some "common grace" that leads us to abandon our

To Accept What We Cannot Change

self-concern, at least partially, for the sake of the wider community.[32]

In 1969, prompted by Richard Nixon's decision to begin holding Sunday worship services in the East Room of the White House, at which ministers from various faith traditions would be invited to preside, Reinhold wrote an essay for *Christianity and Crisis* titled "The King's Chapel and the King's Court."[33] Incensed at the fawning and sycophantic character of the sermons delivered in the President's dwelling, he compared the ministers to Amaziah, the priest in the court of the Israelite king Jeroboam, who commanded the prophet Amos not to prophesy at Bethel "for it is the kings chapel, and the king's court."[34]

Like Amaziah, the minsters who preached in "the king's court" of the East Room, such as Reinhold's nemesis Billy Graham, who inaugurated the program, preferred comforting spiritual platitudes to prophetic utterance about social justice and the Vietnam war. They were "high priests in the cult of complacency and self-sufficiency."[35] These ministers failed to recognize the difference, Reinhold argued, between conventional religion, "which throws the aura of sanctity on contemporary public policy, whether morally inferior or outrageously unjust," and a radical religion that subjects all human institutions and structures to the judgment of God's righteousness.[36]

Amos's prophetic stance was rooted, not in preaching that would please the king and his court, but in the divine demand that all social policy be oriented toward the struggle to achieve justice. Reinhold wondered whether Martin Luther King Jr., had he not been murdered, would have been invited to the august assembly of White House preachers. "Perhaps the FBI, which spied on him," Reinhold notes, "had the same opinion of him as Amaziah had of Amos."[37]

In this essay, Reinhold proved that he still possessed his rhetorical flair, and it may have garnered him more attention than he had anticipated, as Nixon's aide John Erlichman subsequently requested a copy of Reinhold's FBI file.[38] It should also be noted that Ursula, who had become in many ways Reinhold's collaborator and coauthor for much of the work that was written in the last years of his life, played a central role in constructing both the argument and the language of the final essay.[39] Whatever Reinhold may have anticipated by way of response, he was apparently pleased by the volume of hate mail he received as a result.[40]

Another essay from this period bears some attention as well. In 1967 Reinhold wrote "A View of Life from the Sidelines," in which he reflected on his life in the fifteen years since he had suffered his stroke.[41] It offers a poignant reflection on the lessons he took from his last years of life. Considering the two ways in which one finds oneself "on the sidelines"—as an injured player and as a spectator—he

To Accept What We Cannot Change

finds that both of these descriptions suited his situation well. He often felt much like an athlete who had been taken too early from the field, and because of that, he found himself an involuntary spectator of the political and social struggles that had often been so central to his self-identity.

On the one hand, as a spectator, he had a perspective that had been lacking when he was in the midst of the fray, although on the other hand he often felt as though he was failing to exercise political responsibility in his inability to rise to every challenge. However, he consoles himself, the ones that remained central to him—Vietnam and the civil rights movement—were important moral commitments. Movingly, he offers his account of one of the chief lessons that he learned from his disability:

> I learned to know the goodness of men and women who went out of their way to help an invalid. Among the persons who impressed me with their helpfulness were my doctors, nurses, and therapists, my colleagues and friends in the realms of both politics and religion. I soon learned that some of these people

who entered my life professionally, or who served me nonprofessionally with visits and walks, showed an almost charismatic gift of love. And of course, my chief source of spiritual strength was my wife. She was my nurse, my secretary, editor, counselor, and friendly critic through all those years of illness and occasional depression. We had been happily married for two decades, but I had never measured the depths and breadth of her devotion until I was stricken.[42]

Concluding the essay with his reflections on the mystery of the human self and the possibility of life after death, he affirms that "the individual, though mortal, is given, by self-transcendent freedom, the key to immortality. Individual selfhood is not a disaster or an evil. It is subsumed in the counsels of God and enters the mystery of immortality by personal relation to the divine."[43]

To Accept What We Cannot Change

Reinhold was also somewhat amused in these last years to observe the increasing popularity of a short prayer he wrote for a worship service many years earlier at the Niebuhrs' summer home in Heath, Massachusetts, which came to be widely known as the Serenity Prayer.[44] The prayer, which had been included in a Federal Council of Churches prayer book during the Second World War, had taken on a life of its own after being adopted by Alcoholics Anonymous. Reinhold, who had never copyrighted the prayer, was happy to see it put to good use, and he took some wry enjoyment at the various pieces of Serenity Prayer kitsch sent to him by friends and acquaintances. Although popularized in a shorter, and less theologically challenging, form, his original version reads:

> God, give us grace to accept with serenity
> the things that cannot be changed,
> Courage to change the things
> which should be changed,
> and the Wisdom to distinguish
> the one from the other.[45]

CHAPTER SEVEN

The Niebuhr Legacy

H. Richard Niebuhr died suddenly on July 5, 1962, leaving much of his work unfinished. Several of his unpublished manuscripts, such as *The Responsible Self*, were published not too long after his death, while others waited decades to see publication. *Faith on Earth* was ultimately published by his son Richard R. Niebuhr in 1989, while many of his unpublished manuscripts were eventually edited by William Stacy Johnson and published as *Theology, History, and Culture* in 1996.[1]

Reinhold died in 1973, having witnessed the tumult of the 1960s and the beginnings of the social transformations that would transpire during the 1970s. His final publications, as we have seen, continued to demonstrate his talent for the sharp word and the well-placed jab at those in power.

Both brothers have continued to influence theological discourse in the years since their deaths. While the tides of theological fashion have risen and ebbed, the Niebuhrs have been a perennial presence in the conversation about Christian responsibility in public life. They have wielded an influence in the field of theological ethics matched by few others, and while they offered very different analyses of and very different solutions to the pressing issues of Christian morality in modern society, their joint efforts were key contributions to the development of the field of Christian social ethics in the English-speaking world, and their influence has extended far beyond.

Criticisms

No theology with the kind of reach that both Niebuhr brothers' theologies have had can expect to escape all criticism. In Richard's case, one objection pertains to the way in which his "radical monotheism" seeks to dethrone all of the idols of human imagination that we construct for ourselves as repositories of meaning. By rejecting any center of value as ultimate apart from the power of Being itself, Richard's theology risks a kind of "theocide," destroying any possible conceptions of God in the name of the universal principle that lies beneath all of them. "The notion of the one substance or of universal being *can become the most subtle of idolatries.*"[2]

Richard has also been criticized for failing to develop a theory of moral action within his theological ethics. While his approach offers Christians ethics tools for interpreting their moral situations, he offers no method for discerning what choices should be made within the concrete situation.

The Niebuhr Legacy

Thus, while his theology offers important instruments for critical and constructive moral thought, it lacks a usable approach to casuistry.[3]

A widespread and influential criticism of Richard relates to his typology of Christ and culture. Theologians such as John Howard Yoder, William Willimon, and Stanley Hauerwas have argued that Richard's typology is flawed because, while it claims to be a simple description of the various ways in which Christ and culture have interacted with one another in Christian history, Richard displays a clear preference for the conversionist model, through which Christ is seen as transforming culture.[4] By creating a monolithic conception of both Christianity and of culture, they argue, Richard stacks the deck in favor of his preferred model while offering trenchant criticisms of the models he finds less attractive. As a result, the argument goes, Richard endorses a "Constantinian social strategy" that has the effect of endorsing the cultural status quo.[5]

On the other hand, Richard's defenders, such as James Gustafson and William Werpehowski, have argued that this criticism misses key aspects of what Richard had argued in *Christ and Culture*, even to the extent that it may be true he preferred the conversionist model to the others. As Werpehowski argues:

> When Niebuhr talks about history, he allows that a process of mutual correction can, does, and ought to go on among Christians and Christian communities. Radicals keep conversionists from going soft on culture, for instance, whereas conversionists challenge any radical substitution of a new law of cultural life, as if any human attainment is not liable to sin, or as if there is nothing of God's good creation to be found in the world that has been rejected.[6]

Nevertheless, Werpehowski argues, Richard's approach on these issues is at times ambiguous, and his preference for the conversionist model could overcome his attempts to be scrupulously evenhanded. Even so, as Richard makes quite clear in the text, these models are not exclusive, but rather represent intersecting trajectories within the Christian tradition that at their best mutually inform and critique one another.

In Reinhold's case, the criticisms have come from a variety of different directions. Some critics, such as Stanley Hauerwas once more, have argued that Reinhold's theology is not really Christian at all, but rather reflects a form of "religious naturalism" that does affirm the divinity of Christ or the possibility of the resurrection. Hauerwas goes so far as to write: "It appears that for Niebuhr God is nothing more than the name of our need to believe that life has an ultimate unity that transcends the world's chaos and makes possible what order we can achieve in this life."[7] Other

The Niebuhr Legacy

critics have argued that personal prayer and the church as a community of faith played little role in Reinhold's theology. However, as Gabriel Fackre has demonstrated, these criticisms amount to little more than "tall tales" that fail to take into account crucial aspects of Reinhold's life and writing.[8]

To other critics, he was seen as an apologist for power, a cold warrior who wrote for the sake of and in defense of the post-World War II status quo.[9] While there can be little doubt that Reinhold spoke out strongly against communism during the Cold War era, this reading requires one to ignore his repeated and equally strong criticisms of the hubris and self-seeking that the United States risked in taking on a larger set of responsibilities in the world. It also requires one to ignore his late-life opposition to the Vietnam War.

Others, particularly feminist theologians, point out that Reinhold's understanding of the nature of sin was strongly weighted toward the sin of pride and the particularly masculine set of issues that frequently accompanied such an approach. It gave short shrift to the difficulties that women face in a patriarchal society in overcoming systems that force them into passivity and take away their capacity for pride. For women who have been forced into the role of second-class citizens in society, the expression of pride, far from being sinful, can be the result of a decision to overcome the self-denigration that Reinhold associates with the sin of sensuality.[10]

This criticism, while valid in many respects, does not take full account of Reinhold's analysis of sin in *The Nature and Destiny of Man*, which does indeed recognize many of the issues that his feminist critics point to. However, it is at the same time certainly true that Reinhold remained relatively silent on issues of women's power and equality in society.

In a similar vein, some African American theologians, particularly James Cone, have criticized Reinhold for not speaking out strongly enough in favor of civil rights.[11]

The Niebuhr Legacy

While Reinhold frequently wrote of the need to overcome racism and segregation in American society and took pride in his support of the civil rights movement, Cone argues his words seldom translated into concrete action, most notably in his refusal to support a personal plea by Martin Luther King to aid in the civil rights struggle.[12]

These and other criticisms notwithstanding, it remains the case that the Niebuhrs have exercised an enormous influence on theology in the United States over the past half-century, and they have aided in the development of a particularly public brand of theological discourse.

Public Theology and the Brothers Niebuhr

Public theology refers to efforts to articulate the connection between Christian theology and the broader realm of discourse that includes politics, science, art, and other modes of public expression. The Niebuhrs, each in his own way, contributed to the development of public theology as a distinctive approach to theology and ethics within the Christian tradition, connecting the core of the Christian tradition to the pressing questions they confronted during their lives.

Reinhold's theology was always very clearly public in its intention. From his earliest writing, he sought to move beyond the confines of the Christian community in order to address himself to a wider audience, whether it was the German American community on the eve of World War I or the policy makers and politicians in the Cold War era. He worked to make his thought meaningful and accessible to an audience that may not have had much use for his particularly Christian approach to understanding the world. At times, it seems he may have been too successful. Few theologians can claim the dubious distinction of having inspired a group of followers such as the self-proclaimed "atheists for Niebuhr."[13]

While in some of his later writings, such as *Man's Nature and His Communities*, Reinhold had moved away from an explicitly religious interpretation of public life, his public words were always rooted in and returned to the prophetic tradition of the Christian faith. Even when he wasn't using overtly religious language to describe the dynamics of individuals and societies, his thought was always grounded within the predominating Christian themes of sin and grace, irony and tragedy, and love and justice.

Reinhold, as Martin Marty has argued, is the model for what the quintessentially public theologian looks like. Like no one before him, he brought together specifically Christian reflections on morality and public life with a uniquely American form of civic religion[14]:

The Niebuhr Legacy

For all the limits in Niebuhr's observation and despite some hidden ideological biases and tendencies to stereotype, he joined in his person the two main approaches to public theology in America. He took the behavior of his people and, reflecting on it in the light of biblical, historical, and philosophical positions, offered the ensuing generation a paradigm for a public theology, a model which his successors have only begun to develop and realize.[15]

The designation of Reinhold as a public theologian *par excellence* has become widely acknowledged since Marty dubbed him with the title. Larry Rasmussen's widely used anthology of Niebuhr's writings refers to him as a "theologian of public life," while his approach to theology, ethics, and society has been an enormous influence on the subsequent development of public theology as a distinctive discipline.[16]

Apart from Reinhold's influence among policy makers and the political upper class, his influence can be directly felt in Martin Luther King's approach to political strategy

in the civil rights movement. From the beginning, King credited Niebuhr's Christian realism with informing his understanding of both the role of self-interest in the political struggle for civil rights and the moral stakes for the African American communities in basing the fight for civil rights in the philosophy of nonviolence.[17] As King wrote, "While I still believed in man's potential for good, Niebuhr made me realize his potential for evil as well. Moreover, Niebuhr helped me to recognize the complexity of man's social involvement and the glaring reality of collective evil."[18]

Richard's works have made their own contribution to the development of public theology. While Reinhold's approach to the intersection of Christianity and society started with the way in which the major themes of Christian theology could illuminate questions of public importance, Richard started with the church as a distinctive community called to offer a public witness of God's action in the world. However, as James Gustafson has argued, Richard's theology did not end with the church. Rather, radically monotheist theology expresses itself through the myriad publics in which human beings participate:

> Niebuhr, in effect, says that if one wants to write about theology and ethics in relation to science one reads as much as one can, is explicit about one's limitations, and then engages in an interpretation of scientific activity in the light of theology and theological ethics; the same for religion, or for politics, or for academic life in a twentieth-century university. If one chooses to address various academic disciplines and activities, or various aspects of civil society, one finds the points of commonality from which to make theology and theological ethics intelligible, and having done that, one shows how theology can in turn

The Niebuhr Legacy

address these matters not only in negative criticism but also appreciatively.[19]

Public theology, in this sense, is the answer given by Christian faith to the questions raised within the wide array of public realms within which theology participates.

What Reinhold and Richard exemplified in their own approaches to public theology was the way in which the particular elements of Christian discourse can be made meaningful in the context of a larger civic realm. Working from within the Christian tradition and out into the larger complex of issues faced by mid-century America, they provided two distinct and substantive models for how religion can and must relate to the questions of public life.

Conversion, Community, and Theocentric Ethics

Richard's theology attempted to root Christian moral responsibility in the community of faith, which in turn was rooted in relationship to God. And his conception of God was founded on the principle of radical monotheism. While Richard's theology was rooted in a self-consistent conception of the relationship between God, the church, and the believer as a moral agent, many of his successors tended to focus on one or another aspect of his thought in preference to the others.

Paul Ramsey pulled from Richard the particular emphasis on the conversionist model of Christ and culture in the development of his own approach to ethics while also drawing freely on the work of Reinhold, as well as Karl Barth and others.[20] At the same time, Ramsey sought to eliminate the more relativist dimensions of Richard's theology (as in, for example, *The Meaning of Revelation*) in order to provide a stronger set of warrants for Christian moral action.[21] In doing so he appropriates key elements of Richard's theology for the development of his own ethical approach, which he roots in a conception of "covenant love."[22]

Stanley Hauerwas, alternatively, adopts Richard's conception of the church as a community of radical contrast to society as well as his relativism in his own approach to ethics.[23] Taking his cue from Richard's arguments in *The Church against the World*, Hauerwas envisions the church as a community called to witness as a "colony," a "polis" distinct from the values represented by political and cultural liberalism, and to live according to the nonviolent life and teaching of Jesus Christ.[24]

As we've seen, Hauerwas is critical of aspects of Richard's argument in *Christ and Culture*, but his vision of the

The Niebuhr Legacy

church as a community that stands apart from the prevailing values of society and seeks through its witness to testify to another, morally and spiritually better way for Christians to be in the world is one that he shares with Richard. Unlike Ramsey, Hauerwas maintains Richard's emphasis on the relative character of Christian ethics, understanding it in his own fashion as rooted in a narrative and a tradition that are not universal but particular to the Christian community.

Yet a third thread can be traced from Richard's radically monotheistic conception of God to James Gustafson's "Theocentric Ethics."[25] Gustafson argues that Richard's own approach to ethics is thoroughly theocentric. Our moral action in the world is ultimately understood only from the perspective of God's redemptive action in the world. Gustafson writes that Richard's theocentric approach to ethics "is as thoroughgoing as any in recent protestant

theology. Philosophically it can be stated in the following way: the universal is present in every particular."[26]

Gustafson builds on many of the themes of Richard's *Radical Monotheism and Western Culture* in the development of his own approach, which is rooted in a sense of piety toward a transcendent God, and the understanding of all human experience from out of that sense. Morality is ultimately not simply about doing that which is best for ourselves or even humanity, but about conforming ourselves to the will of God. As Gustafson argues, the key moral question is, "What is God enabling and requiring us to be and to do?"[27] As with Richard, this question is rooted in an understanding of God as a center of value that relativizes all other centers of value.

Realism, Morality, and Politics

Reinhold's public influence became more extensive as the idea of "Christian realism" became more prominent. By the post-World War II era, Reinhold had established himself as the leading protestant theologian and ethicist in the United States, and his influence was felt not only through his participation in Americans for Democratic Action and the Council on Foreign Relations, but through his friendships with intellectuals such as Arthur Schlesinger and politicians like Hubert Humphrey.

The key elements of Reinhold's Christian realism had been established as early as *Moral Man and Immoral Society*. His recognition of the power that self-interest and ideology have to undermine the struggle for justice within society while clothing themselves in the mantle of righteousness offered a potent corrective to the complacency of liberal Christianity between the wars. His recognition that human beings were neither wholly corrupt nor completely virtuous

The Niebuhr Legacy

enabled him to avoid the kinds of easy moralism that prevented many of his contemporaries from speaking and acting for fear of staining their moral purity.

Christian realism, as Reinhold formulated it, gave an intellectual foundation for a Christianity that was both morally engaged and politically savvy, which recognized both the risks and limitations of all attempts to act responsibly in the world while at the same time being unafraid to act. Reinhold's insight that the Christian ideal of love transcends all human attempts to realize it in the world does not prevent him from recognizing that the struggle for justice represents the approximation of love within time and history.[28] Political and social responsibility demand that we strive to achieve some semblance of justice in the world, whether that be as in Reinhold's life in the fight to provide decent wages and labor conditions for workers in Detroit's auto plants, the fight to overcome Jim Crow in the South, the struggle to defeat the Nazis in the Second World War or the Communists in the Cold War, or in the need to recognize the degree to which our own overweening sense of national greatness could lead us into tragedy, as in Vietnam.

Reinhold's political eclecticism has led to what some have called his "disputed legacy." Theologians and ethicists on both the political right and the political left have laid claim to the authentic interpretation of Reinhold's legacy.[29] On the left, Robert McAfee Brown's interpretation of Reinhold's thought led him to the support of the theology of liberation in Latin America while on the right Michael Novak became an ardent supporter of the need for "democratic capitalism" and a fierce critic of liberation theology.[30] Both sides of this dispute take hold of genuine aspects of Reinhold's legacy while failing to take account of the whole.[31]

The Niebuhr Brothers for Armchair Theologians

On the one hand, Reinhold was always a supporter of the political left, and the struggle for social and economic justice was never far from the forefront of his concerns. From Detroit to the time of his death, he took great effort to stand on the side of the outcast and dispossessed and had little love for the forces of political conservatism, even in the relatively genial form of Dwight Eisenhower.[32] His last published essay was an attack on the Nixon administration, and in the last decade of his life he spoke strongly against the Vietnam War. In this regard, the partisans of the "liberal Reinhold" read him correctly.

At the same time, the advocates for the "conservative Reinhold" point to his strongly anticommunist stance, his willingness to project American power in international

affairs, and his gradual move toward support for capitalism as evidence that, particularly in the latter part of his life, his realism impelled him more toward the right side of the political spectrum.[33] More to the point, they argue, the political situation of the world after Reinhold's death was different than during his life. Had he lived, they argued, he would have shared their concerns.[34]

Obviously it is impossible to say what Reinhold would have written or said had he lived another decade. However, it is striking that, with the renewed interest in Reinhold's work in the past several years, he has been embraced, not as a "disputed" figure in questions of religion, morality, and public life, but as a figure of common admiration on whom both liberals and conservatives have drawn in order to better understand the ways in which American politics and foreign policies have gone wrong over the past decade. The "disputed legacy" of Reinhold's Christian realism has, over the course of years, transformed into a common moral heritage shared by both left and right.

A Niebuhr Revival

In 2005, historian Arthur Schlesinger Jr. wrote an article for *The New York Times Book Review* titled "Forgetting Reinhold Niebuhr."[35] In the article, he lamented the lack of influence Reinhold Niebuhr exercised on contemporary American political life. Where his name had once been invoked as an authority on religion and politics by advocates across the political spectrum, by the beginning of the twenty-first century, it seemed, he had been relegated to a footnote, sidelined by the influence of the religious right on the one hand and treated as irrelevant by the religious left on the other. "Why, in an age of religiosity," he asked "has Niebuhr, the supreme American theologian of the 20th century, dropped out of 21st-century religious discourse?"[36]

Schlesinger died in 2007, yet since his article appeared, American religious and political life has seen something of a "Niebuhr revival" as Reinhold's influence has once again asserted itself in the aftermath of the disastrous wars and economic catastrophes of the early twenty-first century.

Within a year of Schlesinger's essay, Anatol Lieven and John Hulsman published *Ethical Realism: A Vision for America's Role in the World*, in which they argued for the return of Niebuhrian realism to American foreign policy.[37] Lieven, a political liberal, and Hulsman, a conservative, argued that a bipartisan realist consensus of the kind articulated by Reinhold in *The Irony of American History* provided an antidote to the idealistic hubris of the Bush administration's foreign policy, the results of which had become disastrously apparent by then in Iraq.

Andrew Bacevich made a similar argument in his book, *The Limits of Power: The End of American Exceptionalism*, in which he too argued that the core failure of American foreign policy since the September 11, 2001, attack had been the refusal to recognize the legitimate limits of American power in the world, as well as an arrogant assertion of our own national righteousness.[38] The principle that "you are either with us, or you're with the terrorists," as George W. Bush said in the aftermath of the attacks, coupled with the belief that American military power was sufficient to establish friendly democratic regimes throughout the Middle East, had led us into misbegotten and mismanaged wars from which we could not disentangle ourselves. Bacevich argued for a retrieval of a Niebuhrian sense of humility in international affairs in a way that began to resonate strongly with many Americans for whom the wars in Iraq and Afghanistan increasingly seemed to have been bad ideas.

The Niebuhr Legacy

By the end of 2007, the Niebuhr revival was gathering momentum. The public radio program *Speaking of Faith* produced an hour-long discussion of Reinhold's continuing influence, featuring interviews with several prominent Niebuhr scholars.[39] That April, *New York Times* columnist David Brooks reported on a conversation with an as-yet little-known Illinois Senator named Barack Obama, in which he indicated what he had learned from Niebuhr:

> "I take away," Obama answered in a rush of words, "the compelling idea that there's serious evil in the world, and hardship and pain. And we should be humble and modest in our belief we can eliminate those things. But we shouldn't use that as an excuse for cynicism and inaction. I take away . . . the sense we have to make these efforts knowing they are hard, and not swinging from naive idealism to bitter realism."[40]

Brooks was impressed with Obama's ability to succinctly summarize the central themes of Reinhold's work and became the first of many commentators to link Obama's approach to governance to the work of Reinhold Niebuhr. Reinhold was dubbed "Obama's Theologian," and his influence was divined in many of Obama's policies and speeches.[41] This was particularly the case in Obama's 2009 Nobel Prize acceptance speech, which was widely construed as a Niebuhrian analysis of the challenges of peace in the twenty-first century. While citing the examples of Mahatma Gandhi and Martin Luther King, Obama continued:

> As a head of state sworn to protect and defend my nation, I cannot be guided by their examples alone. I face the world as it is, and cannot stand idle in the face of threats to the American people. For make no mistake: Evil does exist in the world. A nonviolent movement could not have halted Hitler's armies. Negotiations cannot convince al Qaeda's leaders to lay down their arms. To say that force may sometimes be necessary is not a call to cynicism—it is a recognition of history; the imperfections of man and the limits of reason.[42]

Throughout the speech, Obama invoked rhetoric that was clearly informed by a Niebuhrian perspective, arguing that "the instruments of war do have a role to play in preserving peace" while at the same time arguing that war is always a tragic failure to achieve peace on other grounds.[43] The goal of the international community, he argued, was to evolve institutions capable of ensuring greater peace and international cooperation with less use of force over time, but in the recognition that no perfect set of human institutions was possible, and the threat of war was always real. Yet, he continued, it was necessary for us to stretch our moral imaginations to envision greater possibilities for a peace rooted in the ideal of love:

> But we do not have to think that human nature is perfect for us to still believe that the human condition can be perfected. We do not have to live in an idealized world to still reach for those ideals that will make it a better place. The nonviolence practiced by men like Gandhi and King may not have been practical or possible in every circumstance, but the love that they preached—their fundamental faith in human progress—that must always be the North Star that guides us on our journey.[44]

Over the past several years, a steady stream of books on Reinhold's legacy and continuing influence has been published. Among the most significant are Daniel F. Rice's *Reinhold Niebuhr Revisited: Engagements with an American Original*, Andrew Finstuen's *Original Sin and Everyday Protestants: The Theology of Reinhold Niebuhr, Billy Graham, and Paul Tillich in an Age of Anxiety*, Richard Crouter's *Reinhold Niebuhr On Politics, Religion, and Christian Faith*, John Patrick Diggins's *Why Niebuhr Now?*, and Charles Lemert's *Why Niebuhr Matters*. What these volumes share in common is their assertion that Reinhold Niebuhr's theology has lessons to offer contemporary American society and that the failure to heed those lessons has been at the heart of many of the tragedies of the past decade.

It remains to be seen how much impact this "Niebuhr revival" will have on the wider cultural and political currents of the United States today. But for the time being, Reinhold's theology is exercising an influence that is unmatched since his death, and insofar as the insights that his work has to offer continue to provide resources that may aid in the

The Niebuhr Brothers for Armchair Theologians

prevention of more and greater public tragedies, it is testimony to one of Reinhold's most powerful statements:

> Nothing that is worth doing can be achieved in our lifetime; therefore we must be saved by hope. Nothing which is true or beautiful or good makes complete sense in any immediate context of history; therefore we must be saved by faith. Nothing we do, however virtuous, can be accomplished alone; therefore we must be saved by love. No virtuous act is quite as virtuous from the standpoint of our friend or foe as it is from our standpoint. Therefore we must be saved by the final form of love which is forgiveness.[45]

Notes

1. Beginnings

1. Charles C. Brown, *Niebuhr and His Age: Reinhold Niebuhr's Prophetic Role in the Twentieth Century* (Philadelphia: Trinity Press International, 1992), 10.
2. Ibid.
3. Richard Wightman Fox, *Reinhold Niebuhr: A Biography* (Ithaca, NY: Cornell University Press, 1996), 9.
4. Ibid.
5. Ibid.
6. Ibid., 6.
7. Brown, *Niebuhr and His Age*, 12.
8. Fox, *Reinhold Niebuhr*, 12.
9. Jon Diefenthaler, *H. Richard Niebuhr: A Lifetime of Reflections on the Church and the World* (Macon, GA: Mercer University Press, 1986), x.
10. Brown, *Niebuhr and His Age*, 12.
11. Ibid., 15.
12. Fox, *Reinhold Niebuhr*, 16.
13. Ibid., 28.
14. William James, *Pragmatism* (New York: Meridian Books, 1955), 61.
15. Ibid., 133.
16. William James, *The Varieties of Religious Experience* (Oxford: Oxford University Press, 2012).
17. Kevin Carnahan, *Idealist and Pragmatic Christians: Paul Ramsey and Reinhold Niebuhr* (Lanham, MD: Lexington Books, 2010), 16–24.
18. Ibid., 20.

Notes

19. Ibid., 22–24.
20. Brown, *Niebuhr and His Age*, 19.
21. Fox, *Reinhold Niebuhr*, 38–40.
22. Brown, *Niebuhr and His Age*, 20.
23. William Stacy Johnson, "Introduction," in *Theology, History, and Culture: Major Unpublished Writings* (New Haven, CT: Yale University Press, 1996), xiii.
24. Diefenthaler, *H. Richard Niebuhr*, 5.
25. Ibid., 6.
26. Johnson, "Introduction," xiii.
27. Ibid.
28. Diefenthaler, *H. Richard Niebuhr*, 7.
29. Johnson, "Introduction," xiii.
30. Diefenthaler, *H. Richard Niebuhr*, 10.
31. Ibid., 8.
32. Johnson, "Introduction," xiv.
33. Ernst Troeltsch, *The Social Teaching of the Christian Churches*, 2 vols. (Louisville, KY: Westminster/John Knox Press, 1992).
34. Ibid., 993.
35. Ibid, 331.
36. Ibid, 993.
37. Diefenthaler, *H. Richard Niebuhr*, 10.
38. Ibid.
39. Ibid., 11.
40. Fox, *Reinhold Niebuhr*, 41, 62.
41. Reinhold Niebuhr, *Leaves from the Notebook of a Tamed Cynic* (Louisville, KY: Westminster/John Knox Press, 1990), 9.
42. Fox, *Reinhold Niebuhr*, 43.
43. Reinhold Niebuhr, *Leaves from the Notebook of a Tamed Cynic*, 11–12.
44. Ibid., 10.
45. Fox, *Reinhold Niebuhr*, 44.
46. Ibid.
47. Ibid., 46.
48. Brown, *Niebuhr and His Age*, 25.
49. Ibid., 21.
50. Ibid., 22.

51. Ibid., 27.
52. Fox, *Reinhold Niebuhr*, 66.
53. Brown, *Niebuhr and His Age*, 28.
54. Reinhold Niebuhr, *Man's Nature and His Communities* (New York: Charles Scribner's Sons, 1965), 18.
55. Brown, *Niebuhr and His Age*, 25.
56. Reinhold Niebuhr, *Leaves from the Notebook of a Tamed Cynic*, 42.
57. Reinhold Niebuhr, *Does Civilization Need Religion? A Study in the Social Resources and Limitations of Religion in Modern Life* (New York: The MacMillan Company, 1927).
58. Fox, *Reinhold Niebuhr*, 105.
59. Diefenthaler, *H. Richard Niebuhr* 14.
60. Ibid., 15.
61. Ibid., 16.
62. Ibid., 17.
63. Ibid., 18.
64. Fox, *Reinhold Niebuhr*, 123.
65. Ibid., 123–24.
66. Diefenthaler, *H. Richard Niebuhr*, 31–32.

2. The Church in the World

1. H. Richard Niebuhr, *The Social Sources of Denominationalism* (Cleveland: Meridian Books, 1929), 3.
2. Ibid., 6.
3. Ibid., 3.
4. Ibid., 21.
5. Ibid., 18–19.
6. Ibid., 22.
7. Ibid., 237–38.
8. Ibid., 263.
9. Ibid., 279.
10. Ibid.
11. Ibid., 282.
12. Diefenthaler, *H. Richard Niebuhr*, 32.
13. H. Richard Niebuhr, *"The Responsibility of the Church for Society" and Other Essays by H. Richard Niebuhr*, ed. Kristine

Notes

A. Culp (Lousiville, KY: Westminster John Knox Press, 2008), 28.
14. Ibid., 29.
15. Ibid.
16. Ibid., 31.
17. Ibid., 22.
18. Ibid.
19. Ibid., 33.
20. H. Richard Niebuhr, *The Kingdom of God in America* (Middletown, CT: Wesleyan University Press, 1937), xxi.
21. Ibid., xxii.
22. Ibid.
23. Ibid. 43–44.
24. Ibid., 102.
25. Ibid. 130–31.
26. Ibid., 138.
27. Ibid., 160.
28. Ibid., 163.
29. Ibid., 193.
30. Ibid. xxiii–xxiv.
31. Ibid., xxvi.
32. Ibid.

3. Christian Realism

1. Fox, *Reinhold Niebuhr*, 111.
2. Ibid.
3. Brown, *Niebuhr and His Age*, 41.
4. Fox, *Reinhold Niebuhr*, 135.
5. H. Richard Niebuhr, "The Grace of Doing Nothing," reprinted in *War in the Twentieth Century*, ed. Richard B. Miller (Louisville, KY: Westminster/John Knox Press, 1992).
6. Ibid., 7.
7. Ibid., 9.
8. Ibid.
9. Reinhold Niebuhr, "Must We Do Nothing," in *War in the Twentieth Century*, 12. Originally published in *The Christian Century* (March 30, 1932).

Notes

10. Ibid., 15.
11. Ibid., 17.
12. Ibid., 16.
13. Ibid., 17–18.
14. Ibid., 18.
15. H. Richard Niebuhr, "A Communication: The Only Way into the Kingdom of God" in *War in the Twentieth Century*, 20. Originally published in *The Christian Century* (April 6, 1932).
16. Ibid., 20.
17. Ibid., 21.
18. Reinhold Niebuhr, *Moral Man and Immoral Society* (New York: Charles Scribner's Sons, 1932).
19. Ibid., 74–75.
20. Ibid., 75.
21. Ibid., 82.
22. Ibid., 206–7.
23. Ibid., 252.
24. See David L. Chappell, *A Stone of Hope: Prophetic Religion and the Death of Jim Crow* (Chapel Hill: The University of North Carolina Press, 2004), 50–54. See also Martin Luther King Jr.'s discussion of his pilgrimage toward nonviolence in *Stride toward Freedom: The Montgomery Story* (Boston: Beacon Press, 2010).
25. Reinhold Niebuhr, *Reflections on the End of an Era* (New York: Charles Scribner's Sons, 1934), 151.
26. Karl Marx, *The German Ideology* (New York: International Publishers, 1947), 64.
27. Reinhold Niebuhr, *An Interpretation of Christian Ethics* (New York: Harper & Row, 1935).
28. Ibid., 18.
29. Reinhold Niebuhr, *Beyond Tragedy: Essays on the Christian Interpretation of History* (New York: Charles Scribner's Sons, 1937), ix.
30. Ibid., 94.
31. Reinhold Niebuhr, *An Interpretation of Christian Ethics*, 21.
32. Ibid., 31.

Notes

33. Ibid., 62.
34. Ibid., 74.
35. Ibid., 91.
36. Ibid., 124.
37. Ibid., 137.

4. Theology in a World at War

1. Ronald H. Stone, *Professor Reinhold Niebuhr: A Mentor to the Twentieth Century* (Louisville, KY: Westminster/John Knox Press, 1992), 125.
2. Ibid., 124.
3. Fox, *Reinhold Niebuhr*, 187.
4. Brown, *Niebuhr and His Age*, 96.
5. Fox, *Reinhold Niebuhr*, 193.
6. Ibid., 196.
7. Brown, *Niebuhr and His Age*, 101.
8. Charles C. Brown, ed., *A Reinhold Niebuhr Reader: Selected Essays, Articles, and Book Reviews* (Philadelphia: Trinity Press International, 1992), 56.
9. Ibid., 55.
10. Fox, *Reinhold Niebuhr*, 193.
11. Reinhold Niebuhr, *Christianity and Power Politics* (New York: Charles Scribner's Sons, 1940), 7.
12. Ibid., 5–6.
13. Ibid., 15.
14. Ibid., 85.
15. Ibid., 89.
16. Ibid., 200.
17. H. Richard Niebuhr, "The Christian Church in the World's Crisis," *Christianity and Society*, 6 Summer (1941): 11.
18. Ibid.
19. H. Richard Niebuhr, "War as the Judgment of God," reprinted in *War in the Twentieth Century*, 47.
20. Ibid., 51.
21. Ibid., 54.
22. H. Richard Niebuhr, "War as Crucifixion," in *War in the Twentieth Century*, 65.

23. Ibid.
24. Ibid.
25. Ibid.
26. Ibid., 67.
27. Ibid., 70.
28. Reinhold Niebuhr, *The Nature and Destiny of Man*, vol. 1 (New York: Charles Scribner's Sons, 1941), 1.
29. Brown, *Niebuhr and His Age*, 68–94.
30. Langdon Gilkey, *On Niebuhr: A Theological Study* (Chicago: University of Chicago Press, 2001).
31. Ibid., 17.
32. Ibid., 186.
33. Ibid., 219.
34. Ibid., 252.
35. Reinhold Niebuhr, *The Nature and Destiny of Man*, vol. 2 (New York: Charles Scribner's Sons, 1943), 6.
36. Ibid., 35.
37. Ibid., 40–41.
38. Ibid., 43.
39. Ibid.
40. Ibid., 50.
41. Ibid., 56.
42. Reinhold Niebuhr, *The Children of Light and the Children of Darkness* (Charles Scribner's Sons, 1944), xiii.
43. Ibid., 10.
44. Ibid., 41.
45. Fox, *Reinhold Niebuhr*, 234.
46. Ibid., 238.
47. Fox, *Reinhold Niebuhr*, 236.

5. Revelation and Responsibility

1. Diefenthaler, *H. Richard Niebuhr*, 56.
2. James W. Fowler, *To See the Kingdom: The Theological Vision of H. Richard Niebuhr* (Nashville, Abingdon Press, 1974), 5.
3. Diefenthaler, *H. Richard Niebuhr*, 56.
4. H. Richard Niebuhr, *The Meaning of Revelation* (Louisville, KY: Westminster/John Knox Press, 1941).

Notes

5. Roger Johnson, "Troeltsch on Christianity and Relativism," *Journal for the Scientific Study of Religion* 1, no. 2 (Spring 1962).
6. H. Richard Niebuhr, *The Meaning of Revelation*, 5.
7. Ibid.
8. Ibid., 10.
9. Ibid.
10. Ibid., 11.
11. Ibid., 12.
12. Ibid., 21.
13. Ibid. 50.
14. Ibid.
15. Ibid., 52.
16. Ibid., 53.
17. Ibid., 75.
18. Ibid., 87.
19. Ibid.
20. Ibid., 99.
21. H. Richard Niebuhr, *Christ and Culture* (New York: Harper & Row, 1951), 1.
22. Ibid., 40.
23. Ibid., 67.
24. Ibid., 109–10.
25. Ibid., 122.
26. Ibid., 191.
27. Ibid., 208.
28. Ibid.
29. Ibid., 212–13.
30. Ibid., 256.
31. H. Richard Niebuhr, *Radical Monotheism and Western Culture* (Louisville, KY: Westminster/John Knox Press, 1993), 12.
32. Ibid., 13.
33. Ibid., 27.
34. Ibid., 28.
35. Ibid., 29.
36. Ibid., 32.

37. Ibid., 34.
38. Ibid., 37.
39. Ibid., 42–43.
40. Ibid., 46.
41. Ibid., 52.
42. Ibid., 89.
43. H. Richard Niebuhr, *The Responsible Self* (New York: Harper-Collins, 1963), 7.
44. Ibid., 46.
45. Ibid., 42.
46. Ibid., 43–44.
47. Ibid., 57.
48. Ibid., 60.
49. Ibid., 73.
50. Ibid., 88.
51. Ibid., 119.

6. To Accept What We Cannot Change

1. Brown, *A Reinhold Niebuhr Reader*, 76.
2. Fox, *Reinhold Niebuhr*, 240.
3. Ibid., 252.
4. Ibid., 252–53.
5. Ibid., 242.
6. Stone, *Professor Reinhold Niebuhr*, 181–85.
7. Ibid., 185–89.
8. Reinhold Niebuhr, *The Irony of American History* (Chicago: The University of Chicago Press, 1952).
9. Ibid., xxiv.
10. Ibid., 24.
11. Ibid., 23.
12. Ibid., 39.
13. Ibid., 19.
14. Ibid., 74.
15. Fox, *Reinhold Niebuhr*, 247–49
16. Reinhold Niebuhr, *Christian Realism and Political Problems* (New York: Charles Scribner's Sons, 1953).

Notes

17. Fox, *Reinhold Niebuhr*, 257.
18. Reinhold Niebuhr, *The Self and the Dramas of History* (New York: Charles Scribner's Sons, 1955), 4–5.
19. Reinhold Niebuhr, *Pious and Secular America* (New York: Charles Scribner's Sons, 1958).
20. Fox, *Reinhold Niebuhr*, 254–56.
21. Ibid., 266.
22. Ibid., 11.
23. Ibid., 8–9.
24. Ibid., 21.
25. Ibid., 23.
26. Reinhold Niebuhr, *The Structure of Nations and Empires* (New York: Charles Scribner's Sons, 1959).
27. Ibid., 298.
28. Reinhold Niebuhr, *Man's Nature and His Communities* (New York: Charles Scribner's Sons, 1965).
29. Stone, *Professor Reinhold Niebuhr*, 256.
30. Reinhold Niebuhr, *Man's Nature and His Communities*, 31.
31. Ibid., 109.
32. Ibid., 125.
33. Reinhold Niebuhr, "The King's Chapel and the King's Court," reprinted in *Reinhold Niebuhr: Theologian of Public Life*, ed. Larry Rasmussen (Minneapolis: Fortress Press, 1991).
34. Ibid., 270.
35. Ibid., 272.
36. Ibid.
37. Ibid.
38. Fox, *Reinhold Niebuhr*, 289.
39. Rebekka Miles, "Uncredited: Was Ursula Niebuhr Reinhold's Coauthor?" *The Christian Century*, January 19, 2012.
40. Fox, *Reinhold Niebuhr*, 289.
41. Reinhold Niebuhr, "Epilogue: A View of Life from the Sidelines," reprinted in *The Essential Reinhold Niebuhr: Selected Essays and Addresses*, ed. Robert McAfee Brown (New Haven: Yale University Press, 1986).
42. Ibid., 253.

43. Ibid., 257.
44. Elizabeth Sifton, *The Serenity Prayer* (New York: W. W. Norton & Co., 1993).
45. Ibid., 7.

7. The Niebuhr Legacy

1. H. Richard Niebuhr, *Faith on Earth: An Inquiry into the Structure of Human Faith*, ed. Richard R. Niebuhr (New Haven, CT: Yale University Press, 1989); *Theology, History, and Culture*, ed. William Stacy Johnson (Yale University Press, 1996).
2. Libertus Hoedemaker, *The Theology of H. Richard Niebuhr* (Philadelphia: Pilgrim Press, 1970), 157.
3. James W. Fowler, *To See the Kingdom: The Theological Vision of H. Richard Niebuhr* (Nashville: Abingdon Press, 1974), 266.
4. Glen Stassen, Diane M. Yeager, and John Howard Yoder, *Authentic Transformation* (Nashville: Abingdon Press, 1995), 31–90; Stanley Hauerwas and William Willimon, *Resident Aliens: Life in the Christian Colony* (Nashville: Abingdon Press, 1989).
5. Hauerwas and Willimon, *Resident Aliens*, 40.
6. William Werpehowski, *American Protestant Ethics and the Legacy of H. Richard Niebuhr* (Washington, DC: Georgetown University Press, 2002), 111.
7. Stanley Hauerwas, *With the Grain of the Universe: The Church's Witness and Natural Theology* (Grand Rapids, MI: Brazos Press, 2001), 131.
8. Gabriel Fackre, *The Promise of Reinhold Niebuhr*, 3rd ed. (Grand Rapids: Eerdmans Publishing Company), 101–3.
9. Bill Kellerman, "Apologist for Power: The Long Shadow of Reinhold Niebuhr's Realism" *Sojourners* 16 (March 1987), 15–20.
10. Judith Plaskow, *Sex, Sin, and Grace: Women's Experience and the Theologies of Reinhold Niebuhr and Paul Tillich* (Lanham, MD: University Press of America, 1980).

Notes

11. James Cone, *The Cross and the Lynching Tree* (Maryknoll, NY: Orbis Books, 2011), 30–64.
12. Ursula Niebuhr, *Remembering Reinhold Niebuhr: Letters of Reinhold and Ursula M. Niebuhr* (New York: Harper Collins, 1991), 311.
13. Donald Meyer, *The Protestant Search for Political Realism: 1919–1941* (Middletown, CT: Wesleyan University Press, 1988), xx.
14. Martin Marty, "Public Theology and the American Experience," *The Journal of Religion* 54, no. 4 (Oct. 1974): 334.
15. Ibid., 359.
16. Larry Rasmussen, ed., *Reinhold Niebuhr: Theologian of Public Life* (Minneapolis: Fortress Press, 1991).
17. Martin Luther King Jr., *Stride Toward Freedom* (New York: HarperCollins, 1958).
18. Ibid., 99.
19. James Gustafson, "Foreword" in *Radical Monotheism and Western Culture*, 7–8.
20. William Werpehowski, *American Protestant Ethics and the Legacy of Reinhold Niebuhr* (Washington, DC: Georgetown University Press, 2002), 33–50.
21. Ibid., 45.
22. Paul Ramsey, *Basic Christian Ethics* (Louisville: Westminster/John Knox Press, 1950).
23. Stanley Hauerwas, *The Peaceable Kingdom* (Notre Dame, IN: University of Notre Dame Press, 1983).
24. See Hauerwas and Willimon, *Resident Aliens*; Stanley Hauerwas, *In Good Company: The Church as Polis* (Notre Dame, IN: University of Notre Dame Press, 1995).
25. James Gustafson, *Ethics from a Theocentric Perspective*, 2 vols. (Chicago: University of Chicago Press, 1981, 1984).
26. Ibid., 1:55.
27. Ibid., 327.
28. These themes are well discussed in Robin Lovin, *Reinhold Niebuhr and Christian Realism* (Cambridge: Cambridge University Press, 1995).

29. Matthew Berke, "The Disputed Legacy of Reinhold Niebuhr," *First Things* (November 1992): 37–42.
30. See Robert McAfee Brown, *Liberation Theology: An Introductory Guide* (Maryknoll, NY: Orbis Books, 1993); Robert Novak, *The Spirit of Democratic Capitalism* (Lanham: Madison Books, 1990).
31. On the specific issue of the relationship between Reinhold's thought and Latin American liberation theology, see Dennis P. McCann, *Christian Realism and Liberation Theology: Practical Theologies in Creative Conflict* (Maryknoll, NY: Orbis Books, 1981).
32. Sifton, *The Serenity Prayer*, 331.
33. Fox, *Reinhold Niebuhr*, 294.
34. See Jean Bethke Elshtain, *Just War against Terror* (New York: Basic Books, 2003).
35. Arthur Schlesinger Jr., "Forgetting Reinhold Niebuhr," reprinted in *Reinhold Niebuhr Revisited: Engagements with an American Original*, ed. Daniel F. Rice (Grand Rapids: Wm. B. Eerdmans Publishing Co., 2009), 359.
36. Ibid., 360.
37. Anatol Lieven and John Hulsman, *Ethical Realism: A Vision for America's Role in the World* (New York: Pantheon, 2006).
38. Andrew Bacevich, *The Limits of Power: The End of American Exceptionalism* (New York: Metropolitan Books, 2008).
39. Krista Tippet, "Moral Man and Immoral Society: The Public Theology of Reinhold Niebuhr," *On Being* (American Public Media, October 25, 2007), http://www.onbeing.org/program/moral-man-and-immoral-society-rediscovering-reinhold-niebuhr/132/history.
40. David Brooks, "Obama, Gospel and Verse," *The New York Times*, April 26, 2007.
41. For example, John Blake, "How Obama's Favorite Theologian Shaped His First Year in Office," *CNN.com*, February 5, 2010, http://articles.cnn.com/2010-02-05/politics/Obama.theologian_1_reinhold-niebuhr-president-obama-pastor?_s=PM:POLITICS; see also Krista Tippet, "Obama's

Notes

Theologian: David Brooks and E. J. Dionne on Reinhold Niebuhr and the American Present," *On Being* (American Public Media, August 13, 2009).
42. Barack Obama, "A Just and Lasting Peace" (Nobel Prize lecture, Oslo City Hall, Oslo, Norway, December 10, 2009), http://www.nobelprize.org/nobel_prizes/peace/laureates/2009/obama-lecture_en.html.
43. Ibid.
44. Ibid.
45. Reinhold Niebuhr, *The Irony of American History*, 63.

For Further Reading

Books by Reinhold Niebuhr

Does Civilization Need Religion? A Study in the Social Resources and Limitations of Religion in Modern Life. New York: The MacMillan Company, 1927.

Leaves from the Notebook of a Tamed Cynic. Louisville, KY: Westminster/John Knox Press, 1929.

Moral Man and Immoral Society. New York: Charles Scribner's Sons, 1932.

The Contribution of Religion to Social Work. New York: Columbia University Press, 1932.

Reflections on the End of an Era. New York: Charles Scribner's Sons, 1934.

An Interpretation of Christian Ethics. New York: Harper & Row, 1935.

Beyond Tragedy: Essays on the Christian Interpretation of History. New York: Charles Scribner's Sons, 1937.

Christianity and Power Politics. New York: Charles Scribner's Sons, 1940.

The Nature and Destiny of Man: Human Nature. New York: Charles Scribner's Sons, 1941.

The Nature and Destiny of Man: Human Destiny. New York: Charles Scribner's Sons, 1943.

The Children of Light and the Children of Darkness. New York: Charles Scribner's Sons, 1944.

Discerning the Signs of the Times: Sermons for Today and Tomorrow. New York: Charles Scribner's Sons, 1946.

Faith and History: A Comparison of Christian and Modern Views of History. New York: Charles Scribner's Sons, 1949.

For Further Reading

The Irony of American History. Chicago: University of Chicago Press, 1952, 2008. Reprint, 2008.
Christian Realism and Political Problems. New York: Scribner, 1953.
The Self and the Dramas of History. New York: Charles Scribner's Sons, 1955.
The Structure of Nations and Empires. New York: Charles Scribner's Sons, 1959.
A Nation So Conceived; Reflections on the History of America from Its Early Visions to Its Present Power. New York,: Scribner, 1963. With Alan Heimert.
Man's Nature and His Communities: Essays on the Dynamics and Enigmas of Man's Personal and Social Existence. New York: Charles Scribner's Sons, 1965.
The Democratic Experience. New York: Frederick A. Praeger, 1969. With Paul Sigmund.

Books by H. Richard Niebuhr

The Social Sources of Denominationalism. Cleveland: Meridian Books, 1929.
The Church against the World. Chicago: Willett, Clark & Co., 1935. With Wilhelm Pauck and Francis P. Miller.
The Kingdom of God in America. Middletown, CT: Wesleyan University Press, 1937.
The Meaning of Revelation. Louisville, KY: Westminster/John Knox Press, 1941.
Christ and Culture. New York: Harper & Row Publishers, 1951.
The Responsible Self. New York: Harper & Row, 1963.
Faith on Earth: An Inquiry Into the Structure of Human Faith. New Haven, CT: Yale University Press, 1991.

Anthologies and Collections

Brown, Charles C., ed. *A Reinhold Niebuhr Reader: Selected Essays, Articles, and Book Reviews.* Philadelphia: Trinity Press International, 1992.
Brown, Robert McAfee, ed. *The Essential Reinhold Niebuhr: Selected Essays and Addresses.* New Haven, CT: Yale University Press, 1986.

For Further Reading

Culp, Kristine A., ed. *"The Responsibility of the Church for Society" and Other Essays.by H. Richard Niebuhr.* Louisville, KY: Westminster John Knox Press, 2008.

Johnson, William Stacy, ed.. *Theology, History, and Culture: Major Unpublished Writings.* New Haven, CT: Yale University Press, 1996.

Niebuhr, Ursula., ed. *Justice and Mercy.* Louisville, KY: Westminster/John Knox Press, 1974.

Rasmussen, Larry, ed. *Reinhold Niebuhr: Theologian of Public Life.* The Making of Modern Theology: Nineteenth- and Twentieth-Century Texts. Minneapolis: Fortress Press, 1991.

Robertson, D. B., ed. *Love and Justice: Selections from the Shorter Writings of Reinhold Niebuhr.* Louisville, KY: Westminster/John Knox Press, 1957.

Works on Reinhold and H. Richard Niebuhr

Beach-Verhey, Timothy A. *Robust Liberalism: H. Richard Niebuhr and the Ethics of American Public Life.* Waco, TX: Baylor University Press, 2011.

Beckley, Harlan. *Passion for Justice: Retrieving the Legacies of Walte Rauschenbusch, John A. Ryan, and Reinhold Niebuhr.* Louisville, KY: Westminster/John Knox Press, 1992.

Brown, Charles C. *Niebuhr and His Age: Reinhold Niebuhr's Prophetic Role in the Twentieth Century.* Philadelphia: Trinity Press International, 1992.

Carnahan, Kevin. *Idealist and Pragmatic Christians: Paul Ramsey and Reinhold Niebuhr.* Lanham, MD: Lexington Books, 2010

Clark, Henry B. *Serenity, Courage, and Wisdom: The Enduring Legacy of Reinhold Niebuhr.* Cleveland: The Pilgrim Press, 1994.

Crouter, Richard. *Reinhold Niebuhr on Politics, Religion, and Christian Faith.* New York: Oxford University Press, 2010.

Diefenthaler, Jon. *H. Richard Niebuhr: A Lifetime of Reflections on the Church and the World.* Macon, GA: Mercer University Press, 1986.

For Further Reading

Fackre, Gabriel. *The Promise of Reinhold Niebuhr*. 3rd ed. Grand Rapids: Wm. B. Eerdmans Publishing Co., 2011

Finstuen, Andrew. *Original Sin and Everyday Protestants: The Theology of Reinhold Niebuhr, Billy Graham, and Paul Tillich in an Age of Anxiety*. University of North Carolina Press, 2009.

Fox, Richard Wightman. *Reinhold Niebuhr: A Biography*. Ithaca, NY: Cornell University Press, 1985, 1996.

Gilkey, Langdon. *On Niebuhr: A Theological Study*. Chicago: University of Chicago Press, 2001.

Kegley, Charles W. and Robert W. Bretall, ed. *Reinhold Niebuhr: His Religious, Social, and Political Thought*. New York: The Macmillan Company, 1956.

Lovin, Robin W. *Reinhold Niebuhr and Christian Realism*. New York: Cambridge University Press, 1995.

Plaskow, Judith. *Sex, Sin, and Grace: Women's Experience and the Theologies of Reinhold Niebuhr and Paul Tillich*. Lanham, MD: University Press of America, 1980.

Ramsey, Paul, ed. *Faith and Ethics: The Theology of H. Richard Niebuhr*. New York: Harper & Row Publishers, 1957.

Rice, Daniel F., ed. *Reinhold Niebuhr Revisited: Engagements with an American Original*. Grand Rapids: Wm. B. Eerdmans Publishing Co., 2009.

Scriven, Charles. *The Transformation of Culture: Christian Ethics after H. Richard Niebuhr*. Scottsdale, PA: Herald Press, 1988.

Sifton, Elizabeth. *The Serenity Prayer: Faith and Politics in Times of Peace and War*. New York: W. W. Norton, 2003.

Stone, Ronald H. *Professor Reinhold Niebuhr: A Mentor to the Twentieth Century*. Louisville, KY: Westminster/John Knox Press, 1992.

Werpehowski, William. *American Protestant Ethics and the Legacy of H. Richard Niebuhr*. Washington, DC: Georgetown University Press, 2002.

Index

Abalard, Peter, 106
absolute dependence, 126
anthropology, 17, 28
Alexander, Archibald, 38
anxiety, 78, 86–88, 173, 192
Aquinas, Thomas. *See* Thomas Aquinas
Atlantic, the, 14, 16
Augustine, Saint, 112, 137, 138
"Augustine's Political Realism," 137

Barth, Karl, 3, 138, 164
Bethel Evangelical Church, 8, 12–15, 17, 45–46, 147
Beyond Tragedy, 66, 132, 160
Bonhoeffer, Dietrich, 74
Bush, George W., 170

capitalism, 20, 31, 35, 40, 56, 95, 134, 167, 169
center of value, ix, 114–23, 126–27, 154, 166

Christ above culture, 108–10
Christ against culture, 105–7
Christ and Culture, 104–14
Christ and culture in paradox, 110–11
Christ of culture, 106–7
Christ transforming culture, 111–14
Christian Century, the, 15, 16, 20, 50, 51, 75, 144
Christian realism, 45–72, 74, 137, 162, 166–67, 169
Christian Realism and Political Problems, 137–38
Christianity and Crisis, 74, 147
Christianity and Power Politics, 76–80
Christianity and Society (a.k.a. *Radical Religion*), 75–80
church
  as alternative community, 30, 33–35, 53

  captivity of, 31–35
  as community of repentance and forgiveness, 51–53, 56
  as counter-culture, 53
  loyalty to God, 34
  as movement, 42
  revolt against, 31–32
  revolt within, 32–45
Church Against the World, The, 30–35, 42, 51, 164
"church/sect" typology, 10–12, 25–27, 30
Children of Light and the Children of Darkness, The, 92–96
Civil War, 28, 40
coercion, 33, 35, 48, 50–52, 54, 58, 59, 62–63, 79
Coffin, Henry Sloane, 17, 74
Cold War, x, 131, 132, 135, 141, 157, 160, 167
"color line," 28

193

Index

communism, 49, 52, 76, 95, 131, 134–35
  of love, 30
  Reinhold's opposition to, 96, 129
Communist Party, 20, 53, 96, 130
Comte, Auguste, 7
Council on Foreign Relations, 129, 166
culture, 31, 88
  Christ and, 104–14, 139, 155–56, 164–65
  churches captivity to, 32, 35
  liberal, 79
  and prophetic religion, 66
  western, 114–23, 166
cynicism, 83, 93, 94, 95, 137, 171, 172

democracy, 61, 62, 78, 80, 92, 94, 97, 137, 141, 170
Democratic Party, 96
denominationalism, 20, 23–30, 31, 35
Detroit, Michigan, 8, 12–19, 45–46, 47, 167, 168
divine judgment, 34, 36, 39, 41–42, 52–53, 56, 67, 81, 82, 88, 90, 104, 148

Does Civilization Need Religion? 17
Durkheim, Emile, 10

Eddy, Sherwood, 16, 20
Eden Theological Seminary, ix, 4, 5, 8–10, 12, 19–20
Edwards, Jonathan, 30, 38
Eisenhower, Dwight, 139–41, 168
Elmhurst College, ix, 4, 5, 8, 12, 19
empire, 33, 100, 113, 141–43
Epicurianism, 117
equality, 17, 29, 33, 71, 87, 141, 158
ethics, Christian, x, 1, 2, 23, 26, 53, 58, 66–72, 80–81, 85, 92, 106, 154, 160, 162, 165–66
Evangelical and Reformed Church, 19
evil, 26, 38, 40, 59, 69, 70, 71, 76, 77, 87, 89, 90, 92, 102, 110–12, 131, 133–34, 150, 162, 171, 172
existentialism, 117

faith
  double character of, 116
  as fidelity, 116
  in God, 31, 38, 43, 51, 52, 68, 70, 78, 88, 115
  as historically particular, 100
  and reason, 115–16
  social, 117, 119
  as subjective act, 114–16
  as trust, 78, 88, 116, 121, 126, 128
Faith and History, 95
Faith on Earth, 153
fascism, 95, 96
Federal Bureau of Investigation (FBI), 95, 130, 131, 144, 148
Fellowship of Socialist Christians, 80
First World War. *See* World War I
force, 34, 35, 49, 56, 61, 62, 79, 83, 172
Ford, Henry, 16
Freud, Sigmund, 138, 145

Gandhi, Mohandas K., 62–63, 172, 173
German American community, 3, 13–14, 160
German Evangelical Synod, 2, 4, 9, 13
Germany, 20, 73
Gladden, Washington, 19, 40, 41
God
  as absolute, 31, 55, 126

Index

as acting in history, 52–53, 55–57, 80–82, 98, 102, 112, 162
and Caesar, 24
as center of value, xi, 116–120, 126–27, 154, 166
creative action in the world, 67, 112, 133
encounter with, 103, 138–39
faith in, 100, 115, 116, 164
grace of, 69, 88, 92, 110, 114, 151
incarnate in Christ, 34, 104, 107–9
judgment of, 34, 39, 42, 53, 56, 67, 81, 82, 100, 104, 148
and the limits of human knowledge, 98, 99
loyalty to, 33–34
love of, 38, 69, 70, 83, 91, 104, 138, 141
nature and character of, 34, 53, 67, 68–69, 100
as object of inquiry, 114–15
as principle of being, 118–23
revelation of, 70, 84, 89, 91, 92, 98, 100, 101, 103, 104, 120, 121
sovereignty of, 36, 37, 38, 41, 42, 43, 51, 53, 88, 89
as transcending history, 53, 54–56, 77, 166
trust in, 78, 88, 126–28
will of, 68, 166
gospel, 21, 25, 28, 29, 30, 33, 35, 37, 41, 42, 78, 104, 112
grace, 69, 88, 107, 110, 114, 146, 151, 160
of doing nothing, 51–53
as pardon and perfection, 92
Great Awakenings, 38, 39, 40
Great Depression, x, 31, 35, 46

Harnack, Adolf von, 3
Hegel, G. W. F., 7
henotheism, 116–22
historicism, 98
history, x, 28, 36, 42, 62, 66, 68, 77, 99, 100, 101, 135, 138–39, 141, 144, 146, 155–56, 167
and Christian theology, 100–101
and divine power, 88, 112
and human knowledge, 99
and irony, 131–37, 143, 170, 172
meaning of, 52–58, 88-92, 174
United States, 2, 28, 170
hope, 39, 41, 52, 53, 56, 62, 70, 88, 111, 112, 174
human destiny, 88–92, 135
humanism, 35, 40, 119, 143
humanity, 68, 83, 88, 94, 104, 119, 127, 133, 166
as finite and free, 85–86
as lawgiver, 124
as maker, 124
as nature and spirit, 85
as responsive, 124
as social, 124–26, 144, 145, 162
human nature, 76, 84–88, 94, 95, 145, 157, 173

idealism, 7, 16, 18, 34, 36, 47, 49, 52, 55, 57, 60–62, 64, 76–80, 92–95, 171

Index

ideology, 20, 64, 65, 82, 166
idolatry, 31, 36, 117–19, 154
imagination, 86, 102, 154, 173
immortality, 8, 150
injustice, 35, 41, 59, 64, 81, 83, 87–88, 92–93, 113
innocence, 82, 132–35
irony, 30, 40, 87, 109, 146, 160
   and American exceptionalism, 132–35
   definition, 131–32
Irony of American History, The, 131–37, 141, 171

James, William, 6–7, 10
Japan, 50–51
Jesus Christ, 80, 89, 90, 120
   and denominationalism, 24
   cross of, 31, 34–35, 41, 42, 61, 70, 78, 81–84
   ethic of, 66, 68–71, 76
   incarnation, 34
   as revelation of God, 91, 92, 100, 101, 104, 128
   teaching of, 24, 33, 42, 76–78, 93
justice, xi, 16–20, 36, 49, 57, 58, 59, 61–63, 69, 77, 78, 82, 83, 91–93, 104, 113, 136, 139, 140–42, 147, 148, 160, 166
   as approximation of love, 60, 64, 71, 167

King, Martin Luther Jr., 63, 148, 159, 161, 172
kingdom of God, 36, 39, 41, 42, 50, 53, 57, 77, 91, 112
Kingdom of God in America, The, 35–43
knowledge, 7, 98–104
   as an act of faith, 100
   and imagination, 102
   limitations of, 99, 114

labor movement, 19
last judgment, 90
Leaves from the Notebook of a Tamed Cynic, 17–19
legalism, 89–90
liberalism, 2, 70, 134–35, 164
   Christian, 16, 41, 48
   and isolationism, 74
   and sentimentalism, 39, 41, 43, 49, 53, 60, 76, 94, 140
Liberal Party, 96
love, 38, 56–57, 58–66, 85, 104, 107, 111, 146, 150, 164, 168, 174
   as basis for a social ethic, 30, 31, 54, 56, 59–61, 69, 76, 78, 88
   commandment, 118–19
   cross as perfect symbol of, 61, 70, 78, 83
   as ideal, 54, 57, 61, 63, 68–71, 167, 173
   as "impossible possibility," 66, 68–78
   and justice, 57, 64, 77–78, 83, 91, 104, 160, 167
   of neighbor, 30, 78, 104, 119
   perfectionism of, 71, 77, 78, 138, 173
   self-giving, 58, 63, 70, 83
   suffering, 68, 91

Macintosh, D. C., 6–7, 8, 10
Man's Nature and His Communities, 144, 160

Index

Manchurian crisis, 50–51, 80
Manifest Destiny, 40
Marxism, 20, 49, 50, 64, 65, 70, 117, 135, 136
Meaning of Revelation, The, 98–104, 164
messianism, 90, 135
ministry, 4, 12, 17, 18, 19, 90
modernism, 6, 68, 72, 106
monotheism, radical, 114–23, 154, 162, 164, 165, 166
moral action, 52, 57, 63, 71, 125, 154, 165
Moral Man and Immoral Society, 58–66, 64, 71, 93, 132, 166
morality, x, 8, 28, 50, 58, 61, 62, 64, 66, 68–70, 119, 154, 160, 166, 169
  individual vs. social, 58–91, 61, 64
  as response to divine will, 104
Morrison, C. C., 74

nationalism, 30, 35, 40, 56, 95, 97, 117
Nature and Destiny of Man, 84–92, 132, 138, 144, 158

Nazi party, 73, 74, 76, 80, 82, 167
New Deal, 75, 96
New Republic, 14
New Testament, 90
Niebuhr, Gustav, 2–3, 5
Niebuhr, H. Richard
  ambivalence toward World War II, 80–84, 97–98
  childhood, 2–5
  criticisms of, 155–56
  critique of denominationalism, 23–30, 31, 35
  critique of liberal Christianity, 39, 41, 56, 58
  death, 123, 153
  and Eden Theological Seminary, ix, 4, 8–10, 19–20
  and Elmhurst College, ix, 4, 8, 12, 19
  and Ernst Troeltsch, 10, 24–25, 104
  and historicism, 98
  and idolatry, 31, 36, 154
  personal struggles, 97
  role in Evangelical and Reformed Church, 19
  and Walnut Park Evangelical Church, 9

  and Yale, ix, 8, 10, 21, 23, 30, 123
Niebuhr, Hulda, 3
Niebuhr, Lydia, 2
Niebuhr, Reinhold
  analysis of power, 48–49, 58–66, 77, 87–88, 92–96, 132–137, 143, 146, 157, 166, 168, 170
  and Bethel Evangelical Church, 8, 12–19, 45–46
  childhood, 2–5
  collaboration with Ursula Niebuhr, 47, 148
  criticisms of, 156–59
  critique of Christian pacifism, 51, 56, 58, 74–75, 76–80
  critique of Communism, 49, 95, 96, 129, 131, 134
  critique of Eisenhower era, 139–43
  critique of psychoanalysis, 138–39
  critique of idealism, 16, 47–50, 57, 58–66, 76–80, 92–96, 144, 170, 171

197

Index

Niebuhr, Reinhold (*continued*)
- critique of liberal Christianity, 47–48, 49, 53, 56, 58, 59, 61, 70, 74, 76–80, 94, 134, 135, 166
- critique of German Americanism, 14
- critique of perfectionism, 77, 79
- critique of the social gospel, 17, 47–50,
- death, 153
- and Detroit, 8, 12–19, 45–46, 47, 167, 168
- disputed legacy, 167–69
- and Eden Theological Seminary, ix, 4, 5
- and Elmhurst College, ix, 4, 5
- as "establishment theologian," 95, 129
- FBI investigations of, 95, 130–31, 144, 148
- illness, 137, 139, 141, 148–51
- as "Obama's theologian," 171–72
- opposition to McCarthy, 130
- opposition to the Vietnam War, 147, 167, 168
- political campaigns, 46, 47
- and pragmatism, 6–7, 139
- and relativism, 7
- Serenity Prayer, 151
- Socialist Party membership in, 46–47
  - resignation from, 75
- support for World War I, 13
- support for World War II, 73–76
- and Union Theological Seminary, 12, 17, 45, 46, 47, 74, 131, 143
- use of Marxist analysis, 49, 64
- and William James, 6–7, 10
- and Yale, ix, 5, 6, 8, 13

Niebuhr, Richard Reinhold, 10
Niebuhr, Ursula (nee Keppel-Compton), 46–47, 148
Niebuhr, Walter, 3, 8
"Niebuhr Revival," x, 2, 169–74
nonviolence, 30, 46, 63, 162, 164, 172, 173

Obama, Barack, 171–72
optimism, 7, 70, 72, 79

pacifism, 50, 51, 52, 56, 58, 73, 74, 76–80
Page, Kirby, 17
paradox, 55, 64, 85, 110, 146
Pauck, Wilhelm, 31
peace, 17, 40, 41, 67, 69, 73, 113, 172–73
Pharisees, 89
politics, ix, x, 3, 46, 47, 49, 59, 76, 96, 98, 104, 149, 160, 162, 166, 169
polytheism, 116–19
power, 33, 38, 40, 48–49, 58–66, 74, 76–77, 87, 88, 92, 94, 96, 104, 107, 121, 132, 134–36, 142–43, 146, 154, 157, 158, 166, 168, 170
"power politics," 76, 104
Press, Samuel, 4, 5, 8, 9
prophecy, 28, 39, 41, 66, 67, 68, 70, 90, 107, 147, 148, 160
Protestantism, 36–38, 76, 77, 95, 129, 166
providence, 51
Prussian Union Church, 2
psychology, 6, 138, 139

Radical Monotheism and Western Cul-

Index

ture, 114–23, 166
radicalism
  political, 47, 64, 75, 76
  religious, 25, 27, 53, 75, 89, 104, 107, 110, 121, 122, 126, 148, 156, 164
rationalism, 41, 94, 139
Rauschenbusch, Walter, 19, 41
reason, 79, 85, 88, 107, 111, 135, 172
  contextual nature of, 98
  and faith, 115, 116
  and imagination, 102
  in Thomas Aquinas, 109
relativism, 7, 58, 62, 68, 69, 93, 98–101, 114, 117, 119, 164–66
repentance, 30, 38, 51, 53, 56, 70, 82, 84
responsibility, 46, 47, 74, 97, 109, 114, 123–28, 135, 144, 149, 154, 164, 167
Responsible Self, The, 123–28, 153
revelation, 37, 83, 84, 91, 98–104, 107, 164
  as encounter with God, 103
  defined, 101
  and imagination, 102
  and Jesus Christ, 100, 101, 104, 120
  within a particular community, 98, 100, 101, 102
  and radical monotheism, 120–21
  and space-time, 98–99
revolt, 31–35
Ritschl, Albrecht, 3, 107
Roman Empire, 33, 142
romanticism, 32
Roosevelt, Franklin, 75, 76, 96
Roosevelt, Theodore, 3
Russia, 20, 82

Saint John's Evangelical Church, 3, 5
Second World War. *See* World War II
segregation, 28, 29, 159
self, 104, 117, 118, 138–39, 150
  as agent, 124
  as existing in absolute dependence, 126
  as impartial spectator, 126
  as relational, 125–26

Self-deception, 87, 134
Self and the Dramas of History, The, 138, 141
sentimentalism, 39, 53
separatism, 25, 38
sin, 42, 54, 70, 71, 72, 81, 85, 86, 92, 107, 110, 111, 112, 113, 114, 127, 137, 140, 156, 157, 160
  and egoism, 38, 70, 78, 87, 88, 112, 137, 157
  as pride, 87, 88, 158
  as sensuality, 87, 158
slavery, 28, 29, 75, 113, 133
social gospel, 3, 16, 17, 19, 23, 35, 36, 40, 41, 47, 49, 51, 58
Social Sources of Denominationalism, The, 20, 23, 24–30, 31, 33, 35
socialism, 17, 20–21, 46, 47, 48, 61–62, 75, 76, 80, 131
sociology, 1, 10, 23, 24, 104
Soviet Union, 20–21, 130, 132, 137, 141, 143
Stevenson, Adlai, 137
Structure of Nations and Empires, The, 141

Index

Tawney, R. H., 24
Tertullian, 105, 138
theology, vi, ix, x, 1, 2, 4, 8, 17, 38, 73, 80, 98, 106, 107, 109, 114, 123, 154, 155, 157, 164, 166, 173
  and the church, 100
  as a distinctive discipline, 98
  and faith, 100, 115
  liberal, 53
  of liberation, 167
  public, 159–63
  relative to context, 98
Thomas, Norman, 46
Thomas Aquinas, 109, 111
Time Magazine, 95, 129
Tolstoy, Leo, 105
traditionalism, 32
tragedy, 55, 56, 61, 66, 131, 160, 167
tribalism, 146
Troeltsch, Ernst, 3, 10, 11, 24, 25, 104
trust, 78, 88, 101, 116, 121, 126–28

Union Theological Seminary, 12, 17, 45–47, 74, 131, 143
United Nations, 95, 143
United States of America, 2, 12, 15, 20, 21, 26, 28, 63, 76, 129, 132, 136, 157, 159, 166, 173
  and "American exceptionalism," 132
  and colonialism, 133
  democratic character of, 136–37, 141
  as empire, 141–43
  and genocide, 133
  as global power, 134–35
  as innocent nation, 132–34
  limits of power, 132, 135, 136, 170
  possession of nuclear weapons, 129–30, 134, 143
  and slavery, 28–29, 133

values, 78, 118, 146, 165–66
Van Dusen, Henry, 74
violence, 49, 51, 61, 63, 77, 104
virtue, 38, 87, 88, 94, 111, 131, 132, 134, 135
voluntary associations, 11, 25

war, x, xi, 9, 13, 15, 16, 18, 27, 28, 40, 47, 51, 73–76, 97, 98, 113, 131, 134, 135, 141, 146, 147, 151, 160, 167, 168, 170, 172
  as crucifixion, 82–84
  as divine judgment, 56, 81
Weber, Max, 10, 24
Wesley, John, 38
Whitefield, George, 38
Williams, Bishop Charles, 16
World Council of Churches, 95
World War I, x, 9, 18, 27, 160
World War II, x, 151, 157, 166, 167
wrath of God, 42, 107

Yale Divinity School, ix, 5, 6, 8, 10, 13, 19, 21, 23, 30, 123
Young Men's Christian Association (YMCA), 16

www.ingramcontent.com/pod-product-compliance
Lightning Source LLC
Chambersburg PA
CBHW071912290426
44110CB00013B/1364